Also by
Todd Boyd

Young, Black, Rich and Famous:
The Rise of the NBA, the Hip Hop Invasion and
the Transformation of American Culture

The New H.N.I.C.:
The Death of Civil Rights and the Reign of Hip Hop

Am I Black Enough for You?:
Popular Culture from the 'Hood and Beyond

Basketball Jones: America Above the Rim

Out of Bounds:
Sports, Media, and the Politics of Identity

A Connoisseur's Journey
Through the Fabulous Flix,
Hip Sounds, and Cool Vibes
That Defined a Decade

THE NOTORIOUS PH.D.'S GUIDE TO

The Super Fly '70s

Dr. Todd Boyd

HARLEM MOON

BROADWAY BOOKS

NEW YORK

PUBLISHED BY HARLEM MOON

Copyright © 2007 by Todd Boyd

All Rights Reserved

Published in the United States by Harlem Moon, an imprint
of The Doubleday Broadway Publishing Group, a division
of Random House, Inc., New York.
www.harlemmoon.com

HARLEM MOON, BROADWAY BOOKS, and the HARLEM MOON logo,
depicting a moon and a woman, are trademarks of Random House, Inc.
The figure in the Harlem Moon logo is inspired by a graphic design
by Aaron Douglas (1899–1979).

Page 203 constitutes an extension of this copyright page.

Book design by Ellen Cipriano

Library of Congress Cataloging-in-Publication Data
Boyd, Todd.
    The Notorious Ph.D.'s guide to the Super Fly '70s : a connoisseur's
journey through the fabulous flix, hip sounds, and cool vibes that
defined a decade / by Todd Boyd. — 1st ed.
        p. cm.
    Includes bibliographical references and index.
    1. African Americans—Intellectual life—20th century. 2. African
Americans in popular culture—History—20th century. 3. United
States—Intellectual life—20th century. 4. Popular culture—United
States—History—20th century. 5. Nineteen seventies. I. Title.

E185.615.B635 2007
305.896'073009047—dc22
2006035218

ISBN: 978-0-7679-2187-9

PRINTED IN THE UNITED STATES OF AMERICA

10 9 8 7 6 5 4 3 2 1

First Edition

To the memories of

Richard Pryor

Curtis Mayfield

Gordon Parks

Ron O'Neal

James Brown

Eight-track stereo, color TV in every room, and can snort a half a piece of dope every day. That's the American dream, nigga! Well, ain't it?! You better come on in, man.

—Eddie (Carl Lee) talking to
Priest (Ron O'Neal), *Super Fly* (1972)

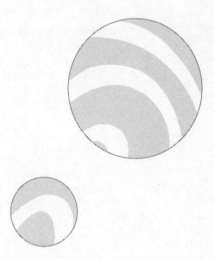

Contents

Part 1

Hot Buttered Soul

AN INTRODUCTION TO THE SUPER FLY '70s   3

Paid the Cost to Be the Boss   3

One Nation Under a Groove:

The Black '70s on Ice   7

Part 2

Hell up in Hollywood

BLAXPLOITATION, WITHOUT APOLOGY   17

Shaft (1971)   23

Super Fly (1972)   31

The Mack (1973)   37

Richard Pryor   43

Pam Grier   51

Bruce Lee 56

Rudy Ray Moore 62

The Spook Who Sat by the Door
(1973) 68

Cooley High (1975) 72

Wattstax (1973) 77

Car Wash (1976) 79

Across 110th Street (1972) 83

Part 3

If You Don't
Know Me by Now

SOUL MUSIC, SOUL POWER 91

Three Kings 96

Marvin Gaye, *What's Going On?*
(1971) 97

Curtis Mayfield, *Super Fly* (1972) 106

Stevie Wonder 113

Aretha Franklin 117

James Brown 123

Quincy Jones 127

Jimi Hendrix, *Band of Gypsies*
(1970) 131

Rick James 134

Barry White 137

Herbie Hancock 139

Al Green 143

The Isley Brothers 144
The Ohio Players 147
Gil Scott-Heron (GSH) 150
Philadelphia International Records 152
"Be Thankful for What You Got"
   (1974) 156
"Smiling Faces Sometimes" (1971) 157

Part 4

Whatcha See Is Whatcha Get

TV AND SPORTS ICONS OF THE
SUPER FLY '70s 161
Didn't I Blow Your Mind This Time?
   Black Athletes Change the Game 167
Sanford and Son (1972–77) 172
Good Times (1974–79) 173
Soul Train (1971–present) 176
Muhammad Ali 179
Julius "Dr. J" Erving 183
Hank Aaron 185
Black Athletes in Hollywood 187
Darryl Dawkins 191

ACKNOWLEDGMENTS 195
NOTORIOUS GLOSSARY 197
WORKS CONSULTED 201

THE NOTORIOUS PH.D.'S GUIDE TO

The Super Fly '70s

PART

Hot Buttered Soul

ISAAC
HAYES
Hot
Buttered
Soul

AN INTRODUCTION TO THE SUPER FLY '70S

PAID THE COST TO BE THE BOSS!

I am a child of the Super Fly '70s. Being born in the six-four, the Year of the Dragon and Muhammad Ali's historic ass whuppin' of Sonny Liston, meant that I would be coming of age, or comin' up, as it were, in the decade that lay ahead. I can't imagine comin' up at a better time.

The '70s—I'll get into the "Super Fly" part later—would coincide with my own tenth anniversary on the planet, and this meant that my experience would evolve right along with everything else. As the Black nation came to life, so would I. I would be growing up during the richest, most fertile period of Black culture ever. The '70s would be the decade that set the tone for all the decades to follow.

Imagine a long, "money green" Cadillac Eldorado, the Biarritz version, a vinyl top of a contrasting color, let's say gold or champagne, you know, "green for the money and gold for the honey," some gangsta whitewalls, with the covered spare tire on the trunk. In my dreams, I'm wearing a slick vine (a great suit) topped off by a pimped-out Borsalino hat, which covers my smooth perm, also known as the "Lord Jesus." As I'm driving, leaning to the side, my eyes level with the steering wheel, an aerosol can of "Money House Blessing" with the Native American head on the side ready to zap any lingering weed smells out of existence, I drive by a powder blue "deuce-and-a-quarter." My eight-track tape player oozes out something laid-back, mellow, and chill. Curtis Mayfield comes to mind. Out of the tinted window, I see people wearing platform shoes, glass heels with dice inside, wild-ass butterfly collars, coke spoons around their necks, the whole nine, straight out of Flagg Brothers or Eleganza, the Black haute couture of the day. This is my fantasy of the era, not one I lived, mind you—back then I was just a li'l shortie myself—but one that I certainly wanted to live, because this was what was around me every day.

When I think about the Super Fly '70s, what always comes to mind is the culture itself: the flix, television shows, fashion, sports, and overall attitude that grows from all of these things. I grew up surrounded by this at every turn. It seeped through every aspect of my life, every pore of my being. I lived it, I ate it, I drank it, I smoked it, and I snorted it. The music was like the sound track, the movies and TV shows provided the visuals, and sports offered the opportunity to see greatness and the never-ending quest to reach a higher level constantly on display.

As a kid, surrounded by all these images of Black culture in the first full decade of a free Black nation, I simply took for granted that it would be this way forever. Things started to change in the late '70s/early '80s; I watched the TV show *Diff'rent Strokes*, heard disco music, and watched Richard Pryor in *The Toy*, and I was suddenly slapped into the reality that all good things unfortunately come to an end.

The early to mid-'70s was the era when Black popular culture exploded in America, a watershed moment when the culture moved from the segregated spaces that it had been forced into, out into the open, now available for a full public viewing.

Black popular culture is no longer confined or segregated as it was back then, but rather it's very much an integral part of mainstream culture in America. There was a time when *Jet* magazine used to list every appearance of every Black person who would be on television for the entire week. To try to do something like this now would require an entire magazine all by itself. We live in a world where Black celebrities host major award shows like the Oscars and the Grammys—often taking home a number of the awards themselves as well. Black celebrities appear on elite mainstream magazine covers, are investors in professional sports teams, head major record labels and flagship fashion outlets on Fifth Avenue, just to name a few things.

Hip hop music dominates the music business in general, while Black athletes have become the norm, providing the standard by which all other athletes are measured. The language of hip hop has entered into the popular lexicon, and hip hop artists, moguls, and NBA players define what it means to be rich and famous for the nation as a whole.

So first and foremost, this book will, like Nas and (his father) Olu Dara, help to bridge the gap between the present and the past. Hip hop didn't just come up out of nowhere on its own. Like all culture, it grew out of what came before it. This book will help you understand how the '70s set the table for the hip hop explosion and how deeply indebted hip hop is to Black culture from that pivotal decade.

The '70s were, of course, significant in their own right long before hip hop came along. Poised between the militant politics of the late '60s and the emergence of the conservative Reagan '80s, the '70s stand as a decade full of any- and everything. Because it was so new, there was a freshness to the culture that came forward, a sense of liberation, a statement of self-determination on the part of all those people who felt that they were no longer going to try to appease mainstream taste. Instead, they were emboldened in their commitment to being as Black as they wanted to be: in style, taste, and overall action. The Blacker, the better. When I was a young kid in the '70s, my aunt bought me a T-shirt with a picture of James Brown rockin' his perfect Afro. This T-shirt said it best: SAY IT LOUD. I'M BLACK AND I'M PROUD.

In one sense, the '70s stands out because there was very little that came before it in terms of consistent mainstream Black entertainment. There was a limited Black presence on television, and a generally stereotypical presence at that. The representation in film wasn't any better, save for Sidney Poitier, who, though highly relevant at one time, eventually wore out his welcome because he was represented as being so perfect that he started to look like a figment of some White liberal's imagination as opposed to a real Black person. While I can most certainly appreciate all his pride and dignity now, there came a time in the late '60s when Poitier just wasn't what was needed anymore. Even Poitier himself realized this when he changed his image in the mid-'70s, teaming up with Bill Cosby in *Uptown Saturday Night* (1974), *Let's Do It Again* (1975), and *A Piece of the Action* (1977).

The '70s represented something bold, something striking, something so far out of the box as to never have been seen or contemplated before for Black culture. The incredible creative energy that emerged from the politics and rebellion of Black America in the late '60s was now being channeled into the music that people listened to, along with the movies and television shows that they watched and the fashions that they wore. There was now a completely different outlook on life that grew out of this newly liberated state of being. The people had thrown off the mental shackles of times past and were embracing the changes that were coursing through the veins of the culture. This was the "brand-new bag" that James Brown had been talking about in his song, and it was also what the Philadelphia group McFadden and Whitehead meant when they sang their anthem "Ain't No Stoppin' Us Now" in 1979. When Charles Wright and the Watts 103rd Street Rhythm Band sang "Express Yourself" (1970), they too were dealing with freedom of expression and self-determination, both ideas that had come to define the '70s.

ONE NATION UNDER A GROOVE:
THE BLACK '70S ON ICE

In the '70s, the decade immediately following the civil rights and Black power movements in America, Black popular culture emerged onto the national scene. This visible emergence began a transformation of American culture that continues to influence what we watch and listen to today. Prior to the '70s, racial restrictions in America generally meant that Black culture was kept under wraps, often operating in segregated environments like the "chitlin circuit," and when visible, the images were generally either stereotypical, nonthreatening, or both. Yet in the 1970s, not only were there a larger number of Black media images now available, but the mode of expression was decidedly much more demonstrative.

Prompted by the politics of the time, Black culture was vibrant, energetic, and responsive to the conditions that were starting to shape a newly emancipated group of people. In the past, a great deal of Black culture that was available to the masses had been specific to White definitions of Black expression. However, in the '70s, Black culture started to assume a "for us, by us" sensibility that allowed for the free expression of a culture that was hip, funky, and interested in its own overall sense of identity.

The '70s represents that point at which Black culture started to become the mainstream of American popular culture at large. And while Black culture had since the 1920s served as the avant-garde of American culture, this culture was now visible in the most mainstream of places and started to define what was hip and cool. This would only increase over time.

One of my favorite flix of all time is the Gordon Parks Jr. masterpiece *Super Fly*, starring Ron O'Neal. To me, that movie was about pursuing life to the fullest, overcoming obstacles, making the best of a bad situation, turning nothing into something, maximizing yourself in one area only to parlay and move into another. On top of this, everything in the flick was just like the title: fly. The clothes, the cars, the dialogue, the whole scene, everything about that movie was so fly that a normal degree of flyness wasn't enough; it had to be Super Fly! This movie was a metaphor for the whole era.

In the Super Fly '70s, Black America kicked in the door of the entertainment industry and went on to forge an indelible imprint on the American psyche that has continually reshaped the way we experience popular culture in this country. While most Black cultural representation prior to the '70s was similar in existence to most Black people at the time—invisible—the seeming onslaught of Black culture in this new era stood out by contrast and exposed the absence of what had not been in place before.

The Notorious Ph.D.'s Guide to the Super Fly '70s is a showcase of this large proliferation of '70s images from my own perspective as someone who both lived through and experienced this culture firsthand, and who later started writing, researching, and making a living explaining this culture to the masses.

If you haven't figured this out already, I *am* the Notorious Ph.D., a lethal combination of intellect and street knowledge, a unique "collabo" between the formal and the vernacular, a Super Fly '70s blaxploitation hero trapped in a professor's body. Welcome to my world!

The guide is my version of the newest/latest. Some people, though none as erudite and fly as your boy, have discussed the blaxploitation films, the soul music, and the popular television programs of the '70s before, but these separate arenas of entertainment have never been conceived of as one cultural movement with various forms of expression. The guide is unique in labeling this a cultural movement and addressing it as a whole, while still focusing attention on the various pieces that make up the sum of its parts.

The Super Fly '70s focused on representation and self-expression, emboldened by the strident politics of Black empowerment that were at the core of this societal moment. There is an overall mood, sensibility, and mode of representation specific to Super Fly '70s culture that grew out of the political concerns of that era, yet this culture has never been properly represented in all its groundbreaking magnitude. As a matter of fact, many people over the years have dismissed the Super Fly '70s as being frivolous and empty. Some have even derided the whole era as negative and argue that many images took Black people backward in time. Fuck that! It's all love from where I stand.

The guide will showcase the '70s and all the things that I consider Super Fly about it, from my informed and highly subjective perspective. Remember as you go forward, this is the Notorious Ph.D's guide, not an encyclopedia, not a comprehensive textbook, or anything else remotely passing itself off as objective. No, this is my muthafuckin' book! What you will read about here are my favorite things, without apology. If you're looking for Diana Ross or Michael Jackson, you're not going to find them here. If you're dying to read about *Sounder* or some other "positive" Black image from the time, you'd better go pick up a *Jet* magazine, 'cause it's not here. This is about urban culture, the more real, the better, as far as I'm concerned. I ain't tryin' to win no NAACP Image Award. I'm just tryin' to keep it real and be cool at the same time.

Consider this book a running commentary, a bomb-ass journal, and a ready compendium of all things that I consider fly about the era. Whenever you need it, the info is right at your fingertips. For all the true '70s heads, this book will remind you of everything that you loved about the era, and for all of you squares out there, this book will take you to school and put you up on what's really hip too.

For generations of people who came of age in the '80s, '90s, and the new millennium, the '70s served as the school that would shape and influence much of what has been created in the time since, replacing the '50s and '60s as the decades that proved most influential on the baby boom generation. The Super Fly '70s—the explosion of Black popular culture—is, in many ways, a bridge that allowed for the transition from that era to today's hip hop generation. Not only is the '70s representative of a generational shift in American culture, but it is also the cultural warehouse that has continually provided inspiration, source material, and a historical reference point for media representation in the most contemporary sense.

I have always said that you judge the significance of an era by the way future generations respond to that which came before them. This is what makes the '70s so fly: the fact that the hip hop generation has drawn such a great deal from the period. The '70s Black culture set the table for hip hop to come along and feast on all the good shit left behind. This is obviously the case in terms of music, but also in terms of things like the return of cornrows as a popular hairstyle, vintage sneakers as a fashion statement, and a red, black, and green wristband for effect. All of these things came from the '70s, and all of them have been recycled by this new generation.

The culture of the '70s has now returned with a vengeance throughout many contemporary examples of popular culture. One has to appreciate '70s culture in order to fully understand the phenomenally popular culture of hip hop today. Hip hop, with its emphasis on the old-school, has done a great deal to reignite interest in the 1970s through references and other direct connections to the era. When many of today's hip hop artists were coming of age in the '80s, the first decade when VCRs were becoming staples in the home, films from the blaxploitation era formed the largest body of work for them to draw on in creating their own sense of identity.

There are numerous rappers who have taken their names from '70s characters: the Notorious B.I.G., aka Biggie Smalls, for instance, took his name from a character in the Sidney Poitier/Bill Cosby film *Let's Do It Again*. Snoop Dogg recently appeared in the film remake of the '70s television show *Starsky & Hutch* (2004) as Huggy Bear, the role created by Antonio Fargas as the pimp/informant whose presence on the show and in ads for the movie was as important to the show's popularity and the current remake as the two title characters. Snoop, the well-known rap icon who helps make the direct connection between blaxploitation and hip hop, also starred as the title character in the film *Bones* (2001), a remake of the original blaxploitation horror film *JD's Revenge* (1976).

Mario Van Peebles's critically acclaimed film *Baadasssss* (2004) even makes the connection across generational bloodlines, as Van Peebles fictionalized his father Melvin Van Peebles's personal struggle in making his revolutionary independent film *Sweet Sweetback's Baadasssss Song* in 1971.

The rapper Foxy Brown (aka Inga Marchand) took her name from Pam Grier, the original Foxy Brown of the '70s, and that era's reigning female icon. A cursory glance at contemporary culture reveals Quentin Tarantino's obsession with blaxploitation and kung fu films of the age, with all of his films being fully immersed in the intricacies of these earlier genres. Tarantino and Grier would hook up for the '70s homage film *Jackie Brown* (1997). The Hughes brothers' underappreciated film *Dead Presidents* (1995) is a virtual love letter to the films of the 1970s in both style and vibe. The film's '70s soul music sound track has to be one of the best sound tracks ever created for a film. The Hughes brothers' acclaimed documentary *American Pimp* (1999) takes its cue from the popularity of '70s films like *The Mack* (1973) and *Willie Dynamite* (1974), along with an overall obsession with the life of the pimp, or simply "the life," that writers like Iceberg Slim and Donald Goines had rendered in print in such books as Slim's *Pimp* (1969) and Goines's *Whoreson* (1972).

The current genre of music often referred to as "neosoul," which would include popular artists like Erykah Badu, D'Angelo, Maxwell, Angie Stone, Jaheim, Musiq, Dwele, and Jill Scott, among others, makes a strong connection with the original soul music from "back in the day" as well. Of course, much of the music that serves as the samples in hop hop comes from this same era of soul music.

Not only have the music, film, and the style of the '70s come back, but in many ways, one could argue that hip hop has been at the vanguard of creating a love of '70s Black culture and an overall sense of retro that seems to define much of popular culture in America today.

*   *   *

That being said, let's make our move to the hall of fame. What comes next is my gallery of what I consider some of the most impressive, inspired, ridiculous, but ultimately Super Fly elements of a bygone era that seem never to go away. So, blaze up and get your mind right. Get in the muthafuckin' groove, baby! In other words, relax yourself, let your conscience be free; then delve deep into the mind of the Notorious Ph.D.

Peace

PART

2

Hell up in Hollywood

BLAXPLOITATION, WITHOUT APOLOGY

Before Blaxploitation, Black representation in Hollywood had either been Sidney Poitier, on a good day, or a series of demeaning stereotypes like Stepin Fetchit and Hattie McDaniel, on a bad day. All that started to change with the release of Melvin Van Peebles's independent film *Sweet Sweetback's Baadasssss Song* in 1971. Van Peebles wanted to capture inner-city street energy on film and make a statement using this medium about the political impact that Black film could have on a larger sense of consciousness in society. Van Peebles's goal was a perfect example of what Black Panther party leader Huey P. Newton wrote of in an extended essay on the political merits of the film, entitled, "He Won't Bleed Me: A Revolutionary Analysis of *Sweet Sweetback's Baadasssss Song.*" Newton's main point in the essay was that in addition to the political struggle being waged at the time, there was also a need to reach the people through culture as well, and in his mind, *Sweetback* fused politics and culture in no uncertain terms.

Yet not everyone was so pleased with the film or many of the Black films of the same ilk that followed it. Lerone Bennett Jr., editor of *Ebony* magazine, wrote a widely read and very critical essay entitled "The Emancipation Orgasm," in *Ebony* (1971), which suggested that the images in *Sweetback* and other films of the time were simply a modern twist on old African American stereotypes, and that the film's negative portrayal was demeaning to Black people. These two poles of opinion, dealing with positive and negative representation reflected in Newton's and Bennett's writings, demonstrate the differences that still engulf the larger Black community around culture and cultural images.

Sweetback was radical for several reasons. First of all, the film is dedicated to "All the Brothers and Sisters Who Have Had Enough of the Man." The opening credits also tell us that the film was "Rated X by an all-white jury." This militant rhetoric also helps to contextualize the revolutionary nature of the film's main character, Sweetback, who got his name from a prostitute when he was a child. The prostitute told him he had a "sweet back" in reference to his sexual skills. Not too many films at the time opened with the image of a young Black kid having sex with a prostitute, so it's obvious right off the bat that Van Peebles was interested in challenging people's complacent views about Black characters in film.

Sweetback makes his living working in a "cathouse," where he performs public sex exhibitions for paying customers. Some racist cops ask the manager of the joint to let them use Sweetback to show their bosses that they've made arrests, and Sweetback ends up handcuffed to a young revolutionary named Mu-Mu. When the cops start to brutalize Mu-Mu, Sweetback drops his normally apathetic demeanor and assists him, and they defeat the cops. Sweetback is now on the run, though, and this is what the rest of the movie is centered around. He relies on the people in the community to help him continue his escape, often having to literally fuck his way out of a situation, even using his sexual skills in a fucking duel with a White chick who is part of an outlaw motorcycle gang.

Sweetback manages to escape but leaves a poignant message at the end of the film: "Watch out. A badass nigger is coming back to collect some dues." Not only was Sweetback able to get away with whuppin' the cops' asses, but he also sent a message that there was more to come. Never in the history of cinema had there been a Black hero who was able to exit a film like this, on his own terms and talkin' shit, to boot. Sweetback resonated with urban audiences who vicariously felt empowered by Sweetback's refusal to submit to the powers that be, instead fighting back against oppression. Sweetback, along with the film's confrontational style and its revenge-fantasy aspect, was the ultimate cinematic expression for the Black power generation.

Another set of inspirational elements of the film were the circumstances of its production. Van Peebles raised the money for the film, investing his own capital and attracting investments from a variety of other people, both common and famous, including Bill Cosby in the amount of $50,000. Van Peebles's ability to raise his own money and get this film made on his own terms suggested that Black filmmakers need not rely on the Hollywood system to have their dreams realized. Like the early twentieth-century Black film pioneer Oscar Micheaux before him, Van Peebles was at heart a hustler, who used his skills in this regard to achieve his artistic vision by hook or by crook. This would later be the philosophy of a new generation of filmmakers such as Spike Lee when initiating a rebirth of Black cinema in the mid-to late '80s.

The success of *Sweetback* also turned heads in Hollywood when the movie industry was experiencing a financial slump. The film, shot in less than three weeks, and which opened in only two theaters, one in Atlanta and one in Detroit, was made for $500,000, but by the end of 1971 it had made $10,000,000. *Sweetback* went on to play in urban theaters throughout the country for audiences who had never really been catered to. The film made Hollywood realize that the Black urban audience was viable, and that this untapped market could provide a nice financial cushion in trying times. Following the formula for *Sweetback*, the studio system began making its own versions of Black films, planting the seeds of what would become the blaxploitation movement, and over a period of time created financial success that sustained the industry.

Blockbusters like *Jaws* (1975) and *Star Wars* (1977) came along in the mid- to late '70s, when multiscreen theaters in malls across the country had become the new movie houses, and soon thereafter the studio system was thriving again, but all of this was after blaxploitation films had put Hollywood back on its financial feet in the early 1970s. Hollywood continues to this day to use this lucrative model for making low-budget Black films targeted at urban audiences.

Shortly after the success of *Sweetback*, the films *Shaft* (1971) and then *Super Fly* (1972) were released, and they both expanded on the same vibe that *Sweetback* had initially exposed, reaching even more of the urban audience and catapulting into the culture at large. Yet not all was well in Hollywood. In 1972, an individual named Junius Griffin, an official with the Hollywood branch of the NAACP, spoke in *Variety* about what he saw as the negative images in *Super Fly*, and he is credited with coining the term "blaxploitation," a merging of *black* and *exploitation*. Griffin was expressing the sentiments of himself and others in Los Angeles, as evidenced by a group like the Coalition Against Blaxploitation (CAB), a collection of civil rights and other community organizations that felt that these films exploited the sentiments of the Black audience for the sake of financial gain. Many Black actors of the period who were just starting to find work after years of being denied a place in Hollywood were obviously put off by Griffin's declaration of their work as being exploitative.

I have always argued that the early films from the blaxploitation period, like *Shaft*, *Super Fly*, and *The Mack*, were more compelling in both style and content than many of the films that came about later on in the cycle, when it was clear that Hollywood was milking this cash cow for all it was worth. The elements of the genre got to be formulaic. The hard-as-nails, sexually potent, mostly male protagonists of these films often exposed "evil whitey" and his Uncle Tom Black sycophants, along with fucking everything that moved, while helping his own community in the process. The plots became repetitive and redundant, and the militant politics of the early films slowly gave way to empty, cartoonish images that were laughable the minute they hit the screen. On the other hand, the prevalence of blaxploitation films offered urban audiences the opportunity to see themselves on-screen and engage in some vicarious revenge against the society and the movies that had oppressed them for so long. It's one thing to talk about the negativity of the images, but we should also focus on the way that these urban audiences actively participated in creating their own meanings out of the films that they saw.

The blaxploitation era offered ample and, at times, empowered representation of Black heroes and heroines who didn't take no shit from no one. Considering that there had been virtually no strong visual representation of Black characters before this time, the images from the blaxploitation era set a new standard. In addition, the images from the films and the larger-than-life spectacle that these movies provided were always fun to watch for me, though in many cases even I have to admit that some of the films did leave a lot to be desired. Hollywood is all about fantasy, however, and what better way to fantasize than to see Black urban life, in all its pimped-out splendor, on the big screen?

❊   ❊   ❊

What follows is a collection of some of my favorite flix and figures from the blaxploitation era. Since *Shaft* and *Super Fly* really set the tone for all that follows, and because *Super Fly* is the namesake for this book, you will read about these two larger-than-life flix first, followed by the highly influential cult classic *The Mack*. The next three selections highlight individuals whose image loomed over the era, beginning with the man who moved freely between flix, recordings, and television, the late comic genius Richard Pryor, followed by the biggest female icon of the era, Pam Grier, my Asian homie Bruce Lee, who was just as much a hero in the 'hood as he was all over Asia, and then that ghetto wordsmith Rudy Ray Moore, aka Dolemite. We move on from there to some interesting flix of distinction, like the underground classic *The Spook Who Sat by the Door* (1973), the wonderful coming-of-age joint *Cooley High* (1975), the documentary *Wattstax* (1973), the crossover *Car Wash* (1976), and finally, one of the truly forgotten but especially tight flix of the era, *Across 110th Street* (1972). Can you dig it?

SHAFT (1971)

Director: Gordon Parks
Studio: MGM

One of the most popular blaxploitation flix ever has to be *Shaft*, the late, great renaissance man Gordon Parks's film. The movie was a huge crossover success, making $12,000,000 within its first year of release. *Shaft* starred Richard Roundtree and spawned two sequels—*Shaft's Big Score!* (1972) and *Shaft in Africa* (1973)—as well as a television show. The film's sound track, by the incomparable Isaac Hayes, is considered one of the best ever, and the single "Theme from *Shaft*" has to be one of the most recognizable songs of all times. Filmmaker John Singleton did a remake of *Shaft* in 2000, with Samuel L. Jackson reprising Roundtree's lead role.

Shaft, who was described on the film's poster as "Hotter than Bond, Cooler than Bullit"—a reference to the character James

Bond, and Steve McQueen's character in the film *Bullit* (1968)—revolves around the exploits of supreme Black private eye, John Shaft, a slick-talkin', badass, well-dressed sex machine who don't take no shit from nobody. He can fight, fuck, and negotiate with the best of them. He could kick your ass or outsmart you with equal precision. Shaft was like an all-powerful urban Black superhero, and this was something that America, Black or White, had never seen on-screen.

Shaft is a man-about-town in New York City of the early '70s. He has connections deep in the Black community, as well as being tight with the cops. Bumpy Jonas, the Black underworld kingpin in the film, played by veteran actor Moses Gunn, tells Shaft that he has got his "other foot in whitey's craw," while Ben Buford, the leader of the film's Black revolutionary group, "the Lumumbas" (a reference to Patrice Lumumba, the former leader of the African nation now known as the Congo Republic) criticizes Shaft for "thinking like a White man." These two comments demonstrate Shaft's place in two different worlds. In spite of this criticism and a working relationship with the cops, Shaft finds a way to help both factions, and he maintains his street cred in the process. He manages to successfully walk both sides of the street, and this is what made him such a likable figure: his infinite ability to transcend the bullshit.

Shaft is also a ladies' man in a major way, as evidenced by the sexual implications of his name. "Theme from *Shaft*" points this out directly in the following lines:

ISAAC HAYES: Who's the black private dick that's a sex
   machine to all the chicks?

FEMALE CHORUS: Shaft

ISAAC HAYES: Damn right!

John Shaft was a major playa, and all of the blaxploitation heroes would follow in his footsteps. Women loved Shaft, and he was an equal-opportunity lover himself. He slept with both Black and White women on the regular. He sarcastically tells Vic, his cop friend, that he is "going to get laid," and then later we see him lying butt-ass naked on his girlfriend's sofa as he greets her accordingly.

He is pursued by a White chick who "chooses" him in a bar. Once at the crib, he leaves to take a shower; she follows and ends up taking a shower with him, only to be kicked to the curb when he has to leave to handle his business. She tells him that he is great in bed, but "shitty" afterward. This becomes a recurring comment in the movie. Shaft is so casual and so unaffected by her presence. In other words, he couldn't give a fuck!

It became common in future blaxploitation films to have heroes who had Black girlfriends whom they loved and, of course, the all-American White women (WW) whom they only fucked and for whom they had no affection at all. The White chicks were always presented as the aggressors too, playing off of that old irresistible "mandingo" stereotype. The brothas had no problem with it, though I'm sure many sistas did! Shaft was a model for the modern Black man, and White chicks on the tip were most certainly a part of the equation. This was about the best revenge you could get on White society, as the thinking was for many at that time.

The great boxer Jack Johnson, the first Black heavyweight

champion, regularly flaunted White women back when one could get lynched for quite a bit less. Jazz greats like Miles Davis also had White women when it was far from acceptable, but that was part of what made it so cool.

There is a certain sexual potency that defined the blaxploitation hero, and there was a requirement that all blaxploitation stars had to have a White woman. Black women were a given, but in the interest of challenging the social conventions of the day, blaxploitation heroes routinely flaunted their relationships with White chicks as a way of demonstrating how cool they were and how much disregard they had for the dictates of the masses. Shaft effectively started this trend in the movies.

This was quite different from the passive relationship that Sidney Poitier had with the White chick in *Guess Who's Coming to Dinner* (1967). What went down in the world of blaxploitation was all about showcasing one of America's biggest taboos around race and sex. Blaxploitation films took delight in upsetting this balance. There were even films like *Mandingo* (1975) and *Drum* (1976), which traced the taboo around interracial relationships back to slavery. In so doing, they attempted to expose the sexual politics around slavery in a most exaggerated, sexual, and highly comic fashion.

Shaft is also as "clean" as a cooked chitlin, and he had a knack for always wearing a fine "leather piece," which is what they call butter-soft leather jackets in the 'hoods of L.A. This is what makes him stand out. The brown, three-quarter-length leather trench coat that he wears at the beginning of the film "sets it off," and the black leather ensemble that he wears in the film's climactic scene holds it down. Shaft also rocks turtlenecks under these leather pieces, and this, too, was a defining characteristic of his unique style, a style that was quickly adopted by Black men across America.

One of the themes in *Shaft* that would become a staple in the blaxploitation genre was the conflict between Black nationalists and Black gangsters over control of the community. In the late '60s and early '70s, groups like the Black Panther party and gangsters like New York City's Nicky Barnes—who served as inspiration for the Nino Brown character in *New Jack City* (1991)—began to assume cult status in many Black communities across urban America. Both the nationalists and the gangsters were seen as Robin Hood–like because they had a take-charge attitude about doing something for the community, albeit with different approaches. This is what you see in *Shaft* in the conflict between Bumpy and Ben Buford. Interestingly enough, the revolutionaries always tend to get the short end of the stick in these confrontations. In *Shaft*, Bumpy tears Ben Buford a new asshole when he critiques his naively idealistic Black nationalist approach to dealing with the problems at hand: "Don't you try to bullshit me, boy. We all on the hustle. I sell broads and dope and numbers. You sell crap and blue skies. It's all the same game."

In addition to the heat that Shaft generated with his cool, laid-back style on-screen, it's also important to point out two other prominent players from *Shaft*, director Gordon Parks and the composer Isaac Hayes.

The late Parks was one of the most distinguished cultural figures ever, having initially distinguished himself as the first Black photographer for magazines like *Vogue*, *Glamour*, and *LIFE* at a time when the average Black person couldn't even get a drink of water. He later wrote an autobiographical novel about his childhood in rural Kansas called *The Learning Tree*. The book was turned into a 1969 film of the same name that Parks also directed. Parks would go on to direct *Shaft*—where he also does a cameo in the role of the landlord whom Shaft encounters when he's searching for Ben Buford—and *Shaft's Big Score!* The *Shaft* franchise helped put the venerable MGM studio back on its financial feet, due to the movies' enormous success at the box office. Later, Gordon Parks would even compose the musical score and create a libretto for a ballet entitled *Martin*, inspired by the life of Martin Luther King Jr., which premiered on PBS in 1990. Parks's ability to move across several different worlds with style, grace, and insight made him a very significant, though often underappreciated artist. For all of his contributions, though, he will always remain large in the annals of American culture. Check out the brotha's work!

I should also point out that the screenwriter for *Shaft*, and the author of the book that the film was based on, was a White writer by the name of Ernest Tidyman. The book *Shaft* and the original script were centered on the activities of a White private detective, but after the success of *Sweetback*, MGM decided to make Shaft into a Black character for the film version, with Tidyman penning the script. Tidyman was also the Academy Award–winning screenwriter for *The French Connection* (1971), a film that shares its love of the New York streets with films like *Shaft* and *Super Fly*. He also wrote the popular Clint Eastwood film *High Plains Drifter* (1973).

The music for *Shaft* is the other part of the equation that made this movie such a phenomenon. Before doing his own albums, like *Hot Buttered Soul* (1969) and *Black Moses* (1971), Isaac Hayes, a musician who cut his teeth at Memphis's famous Stax label, helped to create the incredible vibe that underscores all of the action in *Shaft*. In addition to topping both the pop and the R & B charts, Hayes was the first Black composer to win an Oscar for Best Musical Score. The album also won two Grammy Awards, for Best Score for a Motion Picture and Best Instrumental Arrangement. Hayes rocked the Oscars in '72 with his dark sunglasses, vest of chains, and shaved baldhead well before this became a ubiquitous style. He was so cool that he starred in and did the sound track for the film *Truck Turner* (1974), and went on to have a recurring role in the popular '70s TV show *The Rockford Files*.

Hayes's work on the *Shaft* sound track was so successful that sound tracks by famous Black artists became an integral part of the blaxploitation film. Other superstar artists, like James Brown, Curtis Mayfield, Aretha Franklin, Marvin Gaye, and Gladys Knight, among others, eventually got into the sound track game as well. And though many people know the *Shaft* sound track for "Theme from *Shaft*," the real gem on an otherwise great album is the classic "Soulsville," a meditation on the horrific conditions confronting the Black urban poor. "Soulsville" is similar to other songs about the 'hood during the '70s that used the musical form to address social issues. Some of these songs include Donny Hathaway's "The Ghetto," Curtis Mayfield's "Little Child Running Wild," Marvin Gaye's "Inner City Blues," and Stevie Wonder's "Living for the City."

Hayes appeared in the 1988 blaxploitation parody film *I'm Gonna Git You Sucka*, reminding people of how he repped back

in the day. In the late '90s, Hayes became the voice of Chef on the popular animated TV show *South Park*.

SUPER FLY (1972)

Director: Gordon Parks Jr.
Studio: Warner Bros.

When you're known as the Good Doctor, and one of the things that you specialize in are flix, people always want to know, "What's your favorite movie?" That's the wrong question, really. That's like asking a musician, "What's your favorite note?" or asking a banker which one of the Benjamins in his bank he likes the best. The question requires you to be too reductive and fails to imagine that when you work with something, maybe it is too hard to pick "favorites." Anyway, people always ask and they want an answer. Well, I would have to say my favorite joint of all time, and perhaps the movie that has inspired me the most over the years, is *Super Fly*.

Super Fly is the magnum opus of the blaxploitation era. It is a modern-day meditation on the true meaning of freedom from the perspective of a New York cocaine dealer who goes by the name of Youngblood Priest. Released in 1972, it followed on the heels of Gordon Parks's monumentally successful *Shaft*, and was his son and first-time director Gordon Parks Jr.'s masterpiece. Many people over the years have assumed that the senior Parks directed both flix, but it was the younger Parks who helmed *Super Fly*.

The late actor Ron O'Neal, who got his start acting onstage, played Priest, the main character in the film. However, he is best-known for his cool, laid-back, introspective rendering of a man dealt a jive hand, but intent on making one last major deal so that he can "get out of the life" and pursue the true meaning of freedom without the demands of the 'hood bringing him down.

Priest, though, is stagnated in his attempts to leave the game. On one side he encounters much playa hatin' from his former sidekick–turned-snitch, Eddie, played amazingly by the actor Carl Lee. Lee was a known Black character actor of the time, as well as the son of actor Canada Lee, who appeared in several films, including Alfred Hitchcock's *Lifeboat* (1944) and *Lost Boundaries* (1949). Carl Lee is best-known for his work in the Shirley Clarke independent feature *The Cool World* (1964), as well as for being a friend of jazz icon Miles Davis.

Lee's work in *Super Fly* is nothing short of astounding. He also utters the most famous line in the film. When Priest first announces to Eddie his plan to leave "the life," Eddie chuckles sarcastically and inquires whether some junkies who tried to rob Priest had hit him in the head and knocked him silly. He then proceeds to lay out all the stakes regarding Priest's possible early retirement:

"You gonna give all this up, eight-track stereo, color TV in every room, and can snort a half a piece of dope every day? That's the American dream, nigga! Well, ain't it? You better come on in, man."

Snoop Dogg would famously appropriate this line, changing it up a bit, in the intro on his legendary 1993 hip hop album *Dog-*

gystyle. At the same time the conscious hip hop group Dead Prez would use this very reference, but for completely different purposes, on their 2003 record *Get Free or Die Tryin'*.

The film poster for *Super Fly* shows O'Neal dressed in a mean white suit, with a red turtleneck peeking out underneath, gat in one hand, while his chick Georgia, played by Sheila Frazier, lounges nearby. Priest stands in front of his prize hog, better known as a tricked-out Cadillac Eldorado, which would precede the onslaught of the tricked-out Cadillac Escalade SUV and other vehicles, with twenty-four-inch rims, that dominate hip hop in the early part of the twenty-first century.

In the Super Fly '70s, the hog or "ham samich" was a playa's car of choice, and Priest had one of the flyest ever. In an era before luxury foreign cars signified ultimate status on the streets, there was nothing more fly than to be seen driving a Cadillac, and the Eldo was the prize possession of that line. As immortalized in the line "my El D and just me for all junkies to see," from Curtis Mayfield's *Super Fly* sound track, Priest's distinctive whip went a long way in helping to define his gangsta style.

The white suit on the poster is not worn by Priest in the movie, however, but instead is worn by the character KC, who was not only a pimp in real life, as he played in the film, but also the actual owner of the aforementioned hog that was used in the film as well. Yet Priest was not a pimp in the movie; he was a dope dealer, though because of the poster, many people assume that he made his living pimpin' in the film. There are those who, I'm sure, don't see a distinction between pimps and dope dealers, but in the hierarchy of '70s street culture, there was a major difference. The character Eddie alludes to this in the film when asking about Priest's future direction in life: "What else you gonna do, besides pimp? And you ain't got the stomach for that."

In the modern world of hip hop gangstas, the art of gettin' money often involves cats who engage in a range of illegal activities as they "get their hustle on," but in the '70s there was a strict hierarchy of activities, and one was not to be confused with another. Real pimps made their money pimpin', while dope dealers earned their keep slangin'. So what might seem like minor distinctions now were hard-and-fast rules of the game back in the day.

Which brings us to the film's title, *Super Fly*. The meaning of Super Fly lies in an understanding of that elusive concept of *flyness*, a sense that has long permeated urban culture. If something is *fly*, it is thought to be "bad" or "hip"; in other words, it is the ultimate in cool. So if something is said to be "Super Fly," then it is fly to the highest degree of flyness. It's being fly to the ultimate power. The title gets illuminated in one of the best lines of dialogue from the film, after a potential client samples some of Priest's legendary cocaine. After taking a one-and-one, the gentleman declares, "Man, you always got some super fly shit," expressing his approval of the dope's potency.

In the early '70s, cocaine, or *girl*, was not considered to be as dangerous as it would come to be by the '80s. At the time heroin (pronounced *hair-ron* in the 'hood), or *boy*, was thought to be a societal scourge. Things would change drastically over time, and this would be reflected in films from the '90s like *New Jack City* and *Menace II Society* (1993), and especially in Samuel L. Jackson's career-defining, Method acting tour de force as the crackhead Gator in Spike Lee's *Jungle Fever* (1991). But in the early '70s, cocaine was not thought to be the "helluva drug" that it had become by the time Rick James uttered those famous words on *Chappelle's Show* in 2004.

The cocaine theme of *Super Fly* was challenged by the incredible sound track for the film. Mayfield's meditations on street life ring through loud and clear in what I think is the greatest sound track of all time. The songs are themselves often a critique of what we see going on in the film. Mayfield's lyrics work to provide an extra layer of commentary that hovers just above the film's surface, informing, while extending the social dilemmas that confronted urban America in the early 1970s. Songs like "Freddie's Dead," "Pusherman," and the title track were popular singles. The late rapper Biggie Smalls samples the song "Super Fly" to signal his birth in the introduction to his incredible debut album *Ready to Die*. Many of the other cuts on the *Super Fly* album are just as fly. Songs like "Little Child Running Wild," "No Thing on Me," "Eddie You Should Know Better," and "Give Me Your Love" all work to create a stunning aural component to the film.

"Give Me Your Love," of course, underscores the film's famous extended bathtub love scene between Priest and his fine-ass girlfriend, Georgia. This love scene is one of the most famous sex scenes from the era, so much so that it was also the source for Snoop Dogg's intro on *Doggystyle*.

Mayfield would go on to produce several other significant sound tracks during the blaxploitation era, with some of the top R & B artists of the decade. These include Gladys Knight and the Pips' sound track for *Claudine* (1974), Aretha Franklin's *Sparkle*

(1976), and The Staple Singers' *Let's Do It Again* for the 1975 Sidney Poitier/Bill Cosby film of the same name.

What a lot of people remember about *Super Fly*, though—and many of the films from the era, for that matter—are the pimped-out fashions of the day. Priest is always dap whenever we see him, be it in a slick one-piece black zip-up jumpsuit with a butterfly collar or one of his many Borsalino hats. No playa's wardrobe in the '70s was complete without a chapeau from the famous Italian hatmaker Borsalino. Many of the clothes in *Super Fly* were designed by Nate Adams, who also starred in the film as one of Priest's underworld associates.

THE MACK (1973)

Director: Michael Campus

Studio: Cinerama Releasing Corporation/New Line Home Video

The film from the blaxploitation era that has had the most influence on the hip hop generation is *The Mack*. The title of the film is taken from one of the common street names for a pimp, *mack*, which is derived from the French word for pimp, *maquereau*. *The Mack* is set in Oakland, California, and details the rise and fall of John Mickens, also known as Goldie, an ex-con who returns from prison and decides to ply his trade in the pimp game. Goldie is played by Max Julien, who also starred in the blaxploitation western *Thomasine & Bushrod* (1974), and he wrote the script for the film *Cleopatra Jones* (1973).

Goldie, upon his return from prison, reunites with his

brother, Olinga. Olinga is played by Roger Mosely, who later became quite well-known for his role in the 1980s television show *Magnum, P.I.* Olinga is a Black nationalist who heads a community organization intent on creating a better life for its people. This is in direct opposition to Goldie, who has decided to have a go at making it as a top pimp.

This brotherly conflict comes to a head in the famous "Brother's Gonna Work It Out" scene. Set against the backdrop of the Willie Hutch song of the same name, Goldie and his brother debate which method is best for the community: Black nationalism or underworld activity. Olinga wants to clean up the streets by capturing dope dealers, pimps, and other hustlers who he feels bring down the community. Goldie believes that any real success in the community has to do with making money, and he sees his success in the pimp game as evidence that this is possible.

The title of the song "Brother's Gonna Work It Out" from the sound track suggests that they are going to find a way to come together to work out their differences. This sense was also prevalent in 1990, when the iconic rap group Public Enemy did a song by the same title on their album *Fear of a Black Planet*. Their song had very much to do with their sense of consciousness and Black unity, which reemerged around PE's ascent in the late '80s/early '90s.

The scene itself was referenced in the 1998 film *Belly*, directed by music video auteur–turned-director Hype Williams. Williams is famous for his high-production-value videos for people like the Notorious B.I.G., Busta Rhymes, and the ubiquitous P. Diddy. It was Williams who helmed many of the over-the-top, fish-eye-lens, "shiny suit" videos that helped propel Diddy and Mase into the pop stratosphere in the late '90s.

In *Belly*, rappers Nas (Sincere) and DMX (Tommy Brown) argue over their respective directions in life. Sincere is preaching Black consciousness, while Tommy Brown indulges in the life of crime that he's so comfortable in. Though *Belly* came out some twenty-five years after *The Mack*, it is amazing how the issues at hand remain the same for the hip hop generation as they did for those in the blaxploitation era.

The other famous reference to the "Brother's Gonna Work It Out" scene comes on Dr. Dre's landmark hip hop album *The Chronic*, released in 1992. On the intro preceding the track "Rat-Tat-Tat-Tat," Dre samples Olinga's dialogue from the scene when he tells Goldie that "we need to get rid of the pimps, the pushers, and the prostitutes, and start all over again clean," to which someone loudly responds, straight up, "Nigga is you crazy?!"

The Mack and its emphasis on pimpin' represents an overall fascination with the life of pimps and hoes that started in the late '60s and continues to this day in hip hop culture. Following the release of writer Robert Beck's—aka Iceberg Slim—famous novel *Pimp* in 1969, there was an increasing interest in the sphere of the pimps who populated urban America in an era before dope dealers assumed the top spot in the Black underworld. Many academics, for instance, began doing extensive research into "the life," as it was often called, writing such books as Bob Adelman's *Gentleman of Leisure* (1972) and Christina and Richard Milner's *Black Players* (1973). Most films of the blaxploitation era and many of the popular Black television shows of the day featured pimp characters in prominent roles or for comic relief. Other blaxploitation films that focused on pimpin' include *Candy Tangerine Man* (1975) and *Willie Dynamite*, the latter starring Roscoe Orman, who ironically would later become a regular on the long-running children's educational show *Sesame Street*. The actor Antonio Fargas is probably the most famous of these characters for the work he did in the ABC series *Starsky and Hutch* as Huggy Bear.

The pimp character also made a strong comeback in the late '80s with the emergence of Oakland rapper Todd Shaw, known as Too Short, who, more than any other rapper, defined himself in such a way as to revive the interest in the game. One of Too Short's albums, *Born to Mack* (1989), made a close connection to the pimp life and Short's mission. On his album *Short Dog's in the House* (1990), he did a song called "Pimpology," which sampled dialogue directly from the film to explain the science of pimpin'.

In *The Mack*, though, Goldie is a curious choice for the lead role. Max Julien is a light-skinned actor with a neatly coiffed, blown-out Afro. Based on his appearance, Goldie is what would be described in the streets as "pretty," and he was clearly cast in this role to appeal to potential female viewers. Yet the rules for being a "correct and true" pimp say nothing about being pretty. Goldie comes across as soft, and he is seldom convincing when he must "put his hoes in check" for some infraction. Further, he is surrounded by other figures who help to expose his limitations in a role of this magnitude.

On one hand, there is the character of Pretty Tony, played by actor Dick Anthony Williams, who would also play a pimp in the blaxploitation film *Slaughter* (1972). Pretty Tony is one of Goldie's adversaries in the film, and their clash exposes how unfit Goldie is for his role. Pretty Tony is hard, his lines clever, and his game legendary. Of the many famous lines he drops in the film, my favorite is when he calls out Goldie for being a "shade-tree nigga" and a "rest haven for hoes."

He even goes so far as to call Goldie a "car thief"—a diss that would normally seem tame, but the worst thing you can ever say about a pimp is that he acquired his money and his possessions by means other than pimpin'. A "correct and true" pimp considers any money acquired by means other than from a "bitch's ass" to be something akin to counterfeit. So when Pretty Tony refers to Goldie as a car thief, he might as well have been talking about his mother. A pimp like C-Note in *American Pimp*, for instance, will readily tell you that he "don't steal nuthin' but a bitch's mind." Goldie is further put in his place when Lulu, an old girlfriend who becomes his first ho, tells him that everything he needs to know about mackin' he must learn from her.

Yet it is the appearance of Frank Ward, one of the legendary Ward Brothers from the Oakland underworld, who demands the attention of anyone who watches this film. Frank Ward and his brothers were reputedly one of Oakland's top crime families in the '70s, having made their mark through pimpin'. Ward appears in the film sitting in the barbershop, getting his hair "permed," while Goldie watches in utter amazement. However, unlike either Max Julien or Dick Anthony Williams, Ward is a real pimp whose utterly authentic presence on-screen confers this in no uncertain terms.

The film is actually dedicated to Ward, as the opening credits feature a silhouette of Ward set against a blue screen, accompanied by the words "In Memory of a Man." Ward, according to

Mackin' Ain't Easy, the documentary that accompanies the DVD release of the film, provided the filmmakers with access to the Black Oakland underworld. This private access is especially evident in the spectacular scene in *The Mack* of what I like to call "the Academy Awards for Pimps," the famed Players Ball, where real-life pimps and hoes mingle in with the actors in the film, giving the movie a feel of authenticity that would not have been there were it not for the ghetto pass that Ward provided the filmmakers. Ward was eventually killed during the production of the film as a result of what some suggest was a turf war between himself and Huey P. Newton, leader of the Black Panther party. The film itself was shot on location in Oakland amidst the chaos of turf wars, and these events helped to fuel the sense of realism that exists throughout the movie.

The Mack also featured one of the many stellar performances delivered by comic genius Richard Pryor during the '70s. Pryor plays Goldie's sidekick, Slim. His conversations with Goldie throughout the film are incredible, especially the scene of the two of them in the bar as Goldie declares his intention to dominate the pimp game. Pryor's animated responses convey a street credibility that far transcends acting. Pryor is real as real can get! At a certain point in their conversation, Goldie says to Slim, "You know what bothers me, man?" to which Slim responds in an exaggerated comic tone that is pure Pryor, "What bothers you, nigga?"

Pryor's performance in *The Mack* provides viewers with only a brief glimpse of his comic brilliance. He was eventually fired from the film for his chaotic, drug-fueled, unpredictable behavior on set, which included his pimp-slappin' of director Michael Campus.

The film's sound track was laid down by Willie Hutch, and it remains a classic from the era. There is the aforementioned "Brother's Gonna Work It Out," along with the slowed-down grooves on "I Choose You," which references the words spoken by a ho when she "chooses" a new pimp. The legends live on, too, as Willie Hutch's son, who goes by the names Big Hutch and Cold 187, went on to produce many prominent West Coast hip hop acts, including his work with the group Above the Law.

A strong testament to *The Mack* and its continued longevity can be seen in the way that admitted blaxploitation junkie Quentin Tarantino used the film in his screenplay for *True Romance* (1993). Actor Gary Oldman, who plays a pimp and appears as the quintessential White Negro, rockin' White-boy dreads, confronts Christian Slater while *The Mack* plays on a television screen in the background. Oldman is surprised to know that Slater, who quotes book, chapter, and verse, is as up on *The Mack* as he is. This is definitely an example of when "game recognize game," as they say in the streets.

RICHARD PRYOR

There are few figures more emblematic of the Super Fly '70s than Richard Pryor. To call him a comedian is to limit his impact on the culture at large. He made his mark through comedy, and he

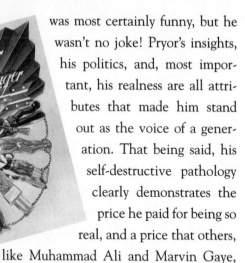

was most certainly funny, but he wasn't no joke! Pryor's insights, his politics, and, most important, his realness are all attributes that made him stand out as the voice of a generation. That being said, his self-destructive pathology clearly demonstrates the price he paid for being so real, and a price that others, like Muhammad Ali and Marvin Gaye, had to pay in their own ways as well. The Super Fly '70s took its toll on those who helped produce such a significant decade worthy of consideration, and unfortunately Pryor's debilitated state during the latter part of his life and his subsequent death are an emphatic demonstration of the attendant casualties.

When Pryor came on the scene in the '60s, he was basically an imitator of the style of crossover comedy made famous by Bill Cosby. One of Pryor's best-known routines during this time was a skit in which he dramatized the birth of a baby. He actually does this bit in his autobiographical film *Jo Jo Dancer, Your Life Is Calling* (1986). As the '60s became more militant, Pryor was starting to feel as though he was suppressing his own voice, and he grew increasingly frustrated with the direction his career was going. One night, while performing in Las Vegas, he had an epiphany and walked off the stage. He eventually headed up to the seat of the counterculture in northern California, settling in Oakland, and became acquainted with Ishmael Reed, the writer, and Huey P. Newton, the leader of the Black Panther party. There is a moment in *Richard Pryor: Live in Concert*, a concert film from 1979, where Pryor recognizes Newton in the audience and asks him to stand up and be acknowledged.

The time spent in Oakland helped to politicize Pryor's material. His comedy now had more of an edge, more fire, and this made the material resonate with the contentious times, especially around the issue of race. Pryor was on his way to becoming a social critic who used the venue of comedy to express viewpoints that were being played out in the streets. This was a far cry from what he did as an imitator of the more mainstream Cosby.

In the early '70s, Pryor began recording on a label called Laff Records. One of the early albums from this label was Pryor's underground classic *Craps (After Hours)*. What is evident here is Pryor's penchant for incorporating the sentiments of the street into his comedy. He was very much an urban comic who was forcing the sensibilities of Black street life onto the agenda, at right about the same time the streets were starting to influence the films of what would become the blaxploitation era. Pryor was like that "nigga in the alley" that Curtis Mayfield talked about on "Pusherman."

This was not hard to do, as Pryor's background made going there so easy. He was born the son of a prostitute and the grandson of a "ho-house madam"; in other words, his grandmother ran the whorehouse that his mother worked in. Given Pryor's upbringing, one can imagine that a certain sense of street knowledge was very much a part of his own cultural DNA. This is why characters like pimps often appeared in Pryor's routines. One of his more famous routines was that of "the pimp on blow," in which he imitated the lyrical musings of a pimp who was high on cocaine. Other street characters, like junkies, winos, and hoes, also became familiar figures in his routines throughout his career.

In 1974, Pryor released his first major label album with the provocative title *That Nigger's Crazy*. This would begin a string of incredible albums that really set the standard for comedy in American culture. These include *Is It Something I Said?* (1975), *Bicentennial Nigger* (1976), and the two-album set *Richard Pryor: Wanted* (1978). This succession of records really defines his body of work and offers compelling reasons as to why he is considered to be the greatest comic ever.

The range of topics on these individual albums moves from his own personal struggles with women and drugs to his unadulterated political musings about racism, along with a smattering of just straight-up comedy. One of the best examples of this can be found in his famous character Mudbone, whom you can hear wax poetic on *Is It Something I Said?* Mudbone was an old Black man who had grown up in Tupelo, Mississippi, and who offered his take on life without compromise. Pryor's intonation and his sly observations made this character come alive as a master storyteller who recounted tall tales from the perspective of a weary but engaged social observer. Mudbone's account about taking his friend to see the voodoo lady, Miss Rudolph, has to be one of the funniest bits ever recorded. His story about the two cats who had a "pissin' contest," over a bridge that ends with the line, "Yeah, and it's deep too," is a good example of Pryor's traditional comedic timing and brilliance, whether he was trying to be political or just trying to be funny.

As you might notice from the title of some of his albums,

Pryor was quite fond of saying the word *nigger,* or what now would be spelled *nigga.* The controversy around this word is such that its frequent use by the hip hop generation constantly prompts debates over whether it is appropriate to say it, and who should be allowed to. No matter what the consensus, its present-day hip hop usage owes a debt to Pryor, whose unabashed utterance of it back in the day liberated the term for future generations.

The word *nigger* and its variants represent the most controversial term in the English language. Once a negative word that was used by racist Whites to insult Blacks, the term has long been a staple of the Black American vocabulary, too. It was generally thought that Black people could use the word themselves, but they did not want to be called that by Whites, though many suspected that White people often used the word in private. The word was generally confined to private conversations, other than among the proud racists who tossed it about as a badge of honor. But Pryor brought it out of the closet in the '70s, as its utterance was essential in conveying the authenticity of the street cats whom Pryor was giving voice to onstage. Pryor used the word so much that over time it started to lose its sting, while still carrying a strong dose of realism whenever it was heard.

To me, what is most important about its usage by Pryor is the fact that he gave voice to a group of people who were otherwise invisible to mainstream society. Pryor humanized the street nigga, and in so doing, he forced America to confront the ugly reality of life for those on the margins of society. Again, this is something that hip hop culture picked up on and took to new levels throughout its very existence.

Pryor also cursed a great deal in his material, and this, too, helped to liberate the language and put forward an assertive view of the way things were from this urban perspective. One of his favorite words was *motherfucker*, which I like to spell *muthafucka*, closer to the way that it should be pronounced. Again, this was emblematic of the language of the streets, and Pryor was intent on bringing this to the public. Bernie Mac, the contemporary comedian, does a hilarious bit on the multiple meanings of *muthafucka* in his segment from the film *The Original Kings of Comedy* (2000). This is without a doubt inspired by Pryor's repeated utterance of the word on his albums and in his stage routines.

Richard Pryor's albums and his stand-up performances were the foundation of his great work, but he also appeared in many films and made several noteworthy television appearances, even having his own variety show on NBC for a short time in 1977. Pryor appears as the comic commentator of all things Black in the documentary *Wattstax*, and his rather brief appearances in films like *Uptown Saturday Night* and *Car Wash* stole the show, and his role as Goldie's sidekick in *The Mack* is nothing short of legendary. Pryor was one of the writers on the Mel Brooks film *Blazing Saddles* (1974), though it is rumored that he was fired from actually being in the film due to some of his violent tendencies during its production. The actor Cleavon Little ended up playing the role originally designated for Pryor.

There are many rumors throughout Hollywood of Pryor's drug-fueled antics and the havoc that he caused during this time in his life. Pryor made a promising dramatic appearance as the star of the film *Blue Collar* (1978), and he also played three different characters in the comedy *Which Way Is Up?* (1977). In

1976, Richard Pryor teamed up with Gene Wilder for *Silver Streak*, the first of many films together, including *Stir Crazy* (1980), directed by Sidney Poitier.

On television, Pryor was originally scheduled to be the host of the inaugural episode of *Saturday Night Live* in 1975, but the network was concerned about the possibility of Pryor saying something that might offend, so he wasn't booked until later in the season. By this time, the network had decided to delay the weekly broadcast for seven seconds to edit any potentially offensive language before it hit the airwaves. When Pryor finally did host the show, his performance helped to make that episode one of the more memorable episodes in the late-night program's long history. Especially significant about this episode was a hilariously classic skit that featured Pryor engaging in an intense game of racial word association with cast member Chevy Chase.

In 1977, NBC debuted *The Richard Pryor Show*. The program format allowed Pryor to demonstrate his comic gifts in a variety of skits that often featured many comics who would eventually become famous in their own right. These include Robin Williams, Sandra Bernhard, Marsha Warfield, and Tim Reid. Pryor's writing partner, Paul Mooney, also appeared on the show. Mooney would have a long career as the reigning consigliere of Black comedians over the years, and he most recently appeared as the character Negrodamus on *Chappelle's Show*.

Throughout the tenure of the short-lived *Richard Pryor Show*, the network was uncomfortable with Pryor's brand of comedy, though they obviously were also intrigued by the show's potential for high ratings based on Pryor's immense popularity. The show was canceled after only four episodes, though Pryor himself claimed that the four shows were the fulfillment of the original agreement. There is a famous skit that was intended for the opening of the show that never aired, but which now appears in the DVD box set for the show.

This skit best explains Pryor's relationship with the network and the censors. Pryor appears speaking directly to the camera, talking about how he didn't have to compromise at all to appease NBC. As the camera pulls back, Pryor is revealed to be naked, and when he says that he didn't have to "give up anything" the camera reveals that he has been physically castrated. Though there are some great moments from the show's short run, Richard Pryor and NBC were far from a perfect fit, as the brilliant comedian was forced to water down his humor for a mass television audience. Were this to have happened today in a television landscape that included cable, Pryor probably could have found a niche for his particular skills, but in the 1970s, when there were only three networks, Pryor was just too radical for such a staid environment.

In 1980, Pryor set himself on fire while freebasing cocaine. He received severe burns that required extensive surgery all over his body. Ironically, this happened at a time when he had started to enjoy great success as a result of crossing over to a more mainstream audience. It seemed as though Pryor's material started to suffer, as the kinder, gentler Pryor was by no means as on point as he had been in the '70s. One of the low points of this downward spiral was his appearance as a human plaything for a young White kid in *The Toy*.

To make matters worse, Pryor announced in *Richard Pryor: Live on the Sunset Strip* (1982) that he would no longer do his famous Mudbone routine; nor would he use the word *nigger* in his routines anymore after coming to a different consciousness while visiting Africa. If there was any question about losing his edge, it was confirmed by comments such as these. The Richard Pryor of the Super Fly '70s was a far cry from the Richard Pryor of the Reagan '80s.

In 1986, Pryor directed and starred in *Jo Jo Dancer, Your Life Is Calling.* The film was a semiautobiographical account of his tortured life. In the early '90s, Pryor announced that he had the disease multiple sclerosis (MS), which confined him to a wheelchair and limited his speech. Later in 1995, Pryor's memoir *Pryor Convictions* explicitly detailed the ups and downs of his storied career. This all seemed like a tragic end to such an important figure, but his influence lives on. Not only was Pryor able to take Black street language and make it mainstream, long before hip hop took it to another level, but Pryor is really the cat who should be credited with initiating the practice of "keepin' it real" as a way of life through his honest, unadulterated performances and lifestyle; again, something that hip hop culture has made an integral part of its very existence.

Richard Pryor died in 2005 from multiple sclerosis.

PAM GRIER

@

One of the biggest icons of the Super Fly '70s has to be the amazing Pam Grier. Her sexy, confident, and larger-than-life demeanor helped to establish her as one of the lasting images from this era.

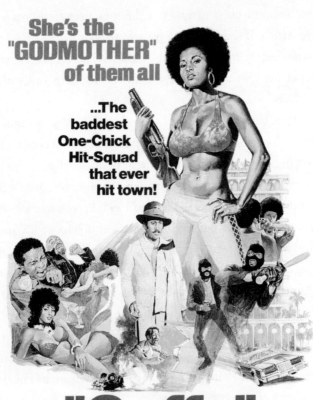

She's the
"GODMOTHER"
of them all

...The
baddest
One-Chick
Hit-Squad
that ever
hit town!

"Coffy"

Samuel Z. Arkoff presents
an American International Picture

starring

"COFFY"

PAM
GRIER ·

BOOKER
BRADSHAW ·

ROBERT
DOQUI ·

WILLIAM ALLAN
ELLIOTT ·

and
SID
HAIG

Produced by Robert A. Papazian · Written and Directed by Jack Hill · COLOR by Movielab

as Vitroni   as Omar

73/157

"COFFY"

The characters that she played tended to be both sexual and smart at the same time, and, if need be, physically adept as well. In other words, she could seduce you or simply kick your ass, and as was the case in several of her films, she might indeed do both. Pam Grier's status in the '70s was such that Quentin Tarantino created his 1997 film *Jackie Brown* specifically for her. Jackie Brown recalls her prowess from the past, while modernizing her image for a more contemporary audience.

Pam Grier's first film was Russ Meyer's *Beyond the Valley of the Dolls* (1970). She later worked with legendary low-budget filmmaker Roger Corman, who cast her in three "women in prison" sexploitation romps: *The Big Doll House* (1971), *Women in Cages* (1971), and *The Big Bird Cage* (1972). Jack Hill directed both *The Big Doll House* and *The Big Bird Cage,* and in 1973 he would direct her in *Coffy,* the first of four blaxploitation features that would establish her image as the female counterpart to dominant male characters like Shaft and Black Caesar.

In *Coffy,* Pam Grier played a nurse who, on her own, goes undercover to enact revenge on the people she feels are responsible for her sister being strung out on heroin. This role would be interchangeable in many ways with the role she played in *Foxy Brown* (1974). Her other films from the era, *Sheba, Baby* (1975) and *Friday Foster* (1975), tended to feature her in similar scenarios as well.

The persona most associated with Pam Grier in these films is that of a very attractive, socially conscious woman who is committed to righting the wrongs in her community. Unlike her male counterparts, who often emerged from the underworld and became Robin-in-the-Hood figures fighting against the evils of a racist society, which often meant the cops, her characters were essentially on the right side of the law and, on some level, determined to do good. For this reason, her character did not have the same complexity as those of her male counterparts. She was much more restrained. Yet in her performances, Grier managed to break away from any potential barriers that may have existed. Her raw sexuality and her incredible screen presence transcended the limited role that defined her character.

In the opening segment of *Coffy* she seduces the dope dealer who supplied her sister with drugs by exposing her abundant chest. As the dope dealer sits transfixed by what he sees, she encourages him to expose himself, only as he goes to do so, she blasts him with a double-barreled shotgun. In the movies of this era, excessive sex and violence were thought to be political commentaries counter to the stifling conservative climate that was overtaking the country. Grier exposes breasts that would certainly be the model for breast augmentation surgery in today's society.

Grier's body is used to seduce one minute, and then in the next minute it might turn out to be the reason that someone gets killed. It's like she possesses the gift and the curse all in the same body. This is her weapon of choice. All the wardrobe pieces that she would wear for these films accentuated her breasts and her body. What was significant about this was that Hollywood, aside from Lena Horne and Dorothy Dandridge, had never considered a Black woman attractive before, but in Pam's movies she was exposing a different body type and redefining the standard of beauty in America. When one considers the rail-thin female aesthetic that dominates today, Pam Grier would probably be thought of as overweight by Hollywood standards. However, she was far from it, and because of her visibility in the '70s, she immediately became the most popular sex symbol for Black men. During this time she appeared in four different *Playboy* pictorials (November 1972, November 1973, December 1973, and December 1976); was on the cover of the popular Black nude magazine from back in the day, *Players*, in December 1979; and became the first Black woman to appear on the cover of *Ms.* magazine in August 1975. These examples demonstrated Grier's appeal to multiple audiences: from nude magazines to feminist publications.

All of her films would involve her sexually charged body, the obligatory catfight, a fight with some hard-core butch lesbians, and some corrupt politicians and maniacal racists. Grier's character is always at the center of these events and manages to emerge on top at the end of the movie, achieving her goal and obtaining a moral victory at the same time.

In the mid '90s, as Tarantino's *Pulp Fiction* (1994) made him one of the hottest directors in Hollywood, he did a *Vibe* magazine interview where he called Pam Grier "the Queen of All Women." In 1997, Grier returned to the screen as the title character in his film *Jackie Brown*. It had been many years since she had burst on the scene with *Coffy*. She was no longer the voluptuous, seductive ass kicker who tore up the screen in the '70s. In addition, much had changed in the political landscape of America and Hollywood since that time, for the worse. So for these reasons, Pam Grier got the opportunity to play a strong female character who used her mind, as opposed to her body, to navigate the film's terrain and still outsmart everyone by the end.

Tarantino is to be commended for creating a star vehicle for a middle-aged Black woman in Hollywood. It is important to remember, though, that this was possible because of her iconic status from the previous era that continued to live on.

Though Grier was the reigning queen of the era, others like former model Tamara Dobson and Teresa Graves also benefited from Grier's popularity. Tamara Dobson appeared in *Cleopatra Jones* and the sequel, *Cleopatra Jones and the Casino of Gold* (1975). Though Tamara Dobson was not nearly as popular as Pam Grier, *Cleopatra Jones* was, for a time, quite popular, though Dobson was never represented in as sexual a manner as her counterpart, Pam Grier. The popularity of both these actresses and their respective vehicles spawned *Get Christie Love!*, starring Teresa Graves, a 1974 made-for-television movie about a Black female cop who clearly came out of the Grier/Dobson mold but was toned way down for network television. *Get Christie Love!* became a network series for ABC, but lasted for only the 1974–75 season. The main character, Christie Love, would often arrest people with the line, "You're under arrest, sugah," a reference that Tarantino used in his first film, *Reservoir Dogs* (1992).

BRUCE LEE

Be like water. Empty your mind. Be formless, shapeless, like water. If you put water into a cup, it becomes the cup. You put water into a bottle and it becomes the bottle. You put it in a teapot, it becomes the teapot. Now, water can flow or it can crash. Be water, my friend.

—BRUCE LEE

Okay, off the top, this is a celebration of one of the greatest niggaz of all time, the legendary Bruce Lee. Even though the majority of the flix from the '70s that inspired this book were blaxploitation films, I have to show love to the other genre that often played in the same urban theaters as the blaxploitation joints did back in the day: martial arts, or, what some would call kung fu films. It would become impossible to talk about kung fu without talking about the man who made this Asian genre popular in America, and that man, of course, is Bruce Lee.

The child of a Chinese opera singer, Bruce Lee was born in San Francisco in 1940, grew up in Hong Kong, went to high school and college in Seattle, and initially began making a name for himself through his martial arts studios in Oakland and L.A. He was a child actor who would later appear as Kato in *The Green Hornet* television series. Bruce conceived of the idea that eventually became the television show *Kung Fu*, but the network was uncomfortable having an Asian actor play the lead, so they decided to use David Carradine, a White actor, instead. It was after this racist snub that Bruce decided to go back to Hong Kong and began creating his own cinematic legend there in films like 1971's *The Big Boss* (aka *Fists of Fury*), 1972's *Fists of Fury* (aka *The Chinese Connection*), and, my personal favorite, 1972's *Way of the Dragon* (aka *Return of the Dragon*).

Bruce died about three weeks before the release of *Enter the Dragon* (1973). This Warner Brothers release is his only Hollywood film, and the first martial arts film ever made by a Hollywood studio. Bruce was working on a film entitled *The Game of Death* when he died of a cerebral edema in 1973. This was listed as the official cause of death, though rumors, myths, speculations, and urban legends have long circulated as to the real reason for his death. Some rumors have suggested that he was murdered by organized crime figures in Hong Kong, known as the triads, for refusing to submit to their extortion attempts; others have suggested that he overdosed on drugs, that he died while having sex with Taiwanese actress Betty Ting Pei, whose apartment he was at when he died, or that at birth he was destined to die based on a long-standing family curse. This last rumor regarding the curse regained steam when his son Brandon died in a shooting accident during the filming of his movie *The Crow* in 1993.

Game of Death was a film in which Bruce was the lead actor, director, writer, producer, and fight sequence choreographer— and he did all of his own stunts. So when he died, the prospects of finishing the film seemed remote, because Bruce had assumed so many roles. The 1978 version of *Game of Death* that was actually released was wack. It used a body double for many of the scenes, along with footage of Bruce from earlier in his career, and generally offered a laughable version of Bruce's true vision for the film. It was only with the discovery of lost footage and the restoration of this footage by John Little in accordance with Bruce's original notes, featured on the documentary *Bruce Lee: A Warrior's Journey* (2000), that viewers had an opportunity to see a glimpse of what he had in mind when making this landmark film.

The plot for *Game of Death* was set around a pagoda in which each of the five floors of the building housed a kung fu fighter using a different style of martial arts. Bruce had to make it from the bottom floor up to the top, while encountering each of these different fighting styles, only to reach the top floor and find NBA legend Kareem Abdul-Jabbar, who was in reality one of Bruce's former students. Aside from the obvious height difference between Kareem and Bruce, Kareem represented Lee's own brand of martial arts, Jeet Kune Do, also known as "the Way of the Intercepting Fist."

Bruce believed that fighting styles were constraining, and Jeet Kune Do was representative of Bruce's Zen beliefs, those being "style as no style." Having originally learned to fight in the streets of Hong Kong, Bruce learned early on that style was no good in the free-flowing world of street fights, where anything goes. He took this thought with him into adulthood, as he went about developing Jeet Kune Do.

Bruce also relied heavily on appropriating other forms he thought to be useful to him and fusing these into his own unique approach. He borrowed strategies from the world of European fencing, as well as from American boxing. He was quite taken by Muhammad Ali, often appropriating Ali's footwork and trash-talking in his martial arts. There's a great example of this in the legendary fight scene between Bruce and Chuck Norris in *Way of the Dragon*. He also drew ideas from Newtonian physics and was heavily influenced by Buddhism and Taoism, along with the teachings of thinkers like Jiddu Krishnamurti. Though many regard Bruce only as a kung fu fighter, he was so much more than that. He was an intellectual and an artist who found his voice and vehicle of expression to be his own form of martial arts.

Enter the Dragon features Bruce, along with costars John Saxon and Jim Kelly. Kelly was an African American martial arts expert who will forever be known as the brotha in *Enter the Dragon*. Though he played the most stereotypical role one could imagine and was killed in a most fucked-up fashion by being lowered into a vat of acid, his presence in the film made him into one of the most visible icons of the blaxploitation era. Kelly, known and recognized for his ever-so-perfect 'fro, went on to star in *Black Belt Jones* (1974) and costar in the film *Three the Hard Way* (1974) with Jim Brown and Fred Williamson. Kelly most recently resurfaced in a LeBron James Nike commercial in 2004, reprising his image from the '70s as an old-school martial arts cat in the modern era.

In *Enter the Dragon*, Bruce, Kelly, and Saxon were lured to an island to fight in a tournament that turns out to be a setup orchestrated by the evil mastermind Han. The climax of the film features Han, now wearing an iron claw for a hand, taking on Bruce in a hall of mirrors. This is an incredible scene, and Bruce, of course, finally kills his nemesis in dramatic fashion.

There was a great deal of interest in martial arts throughout the Black community in the '70s, and the popularity of Bruce Lee had a lot to do with that. As I mentioned earlier, kung fu films played in the same urban theaters as did blaxploitation films, often as a part of double and triple features. There were martial arts studios popping up all over the 'hood, with self-defense being a high priority. Martial arts weapons like the nunchaku—or *nonechucks,* as they were called in the 'hood—seemed to be everywhere at the time.

The most obvious example of martial arts seeping into the public consciousness, though, had to be one-hit wonder Carl Douglas's famous 1974 hit single "Kung Fu Fighting." The song was originally recorded as sort of a joke. It was a throwaway B side recorded when the singer had only ten minutes of studio time left in his session. Though a corny-ass song if ever there was one, the record made it to number one on the *Billboard* charts and had a widespread novelty appeal. Although far less serious than anything Bruce ever did, people still remember it today for its exaggerated sound effects: "Oh-ho-ho-ho—ha!"

Bruce Lee's continued influence on the culture some thirty-plus years after his death is quite evident. There is the phenomenal global success of Jackie Chan, an extra in *Enter the Dragon* who went on to become popular worldwide for his fusion of martial arts and comedy. Chan claims to have created his on-screen persona in an attempt to distinguish himself from Bruce Lee. Whereas Bruce's characters were always hard and serious, Chan's performances are geared more toward comedy, where the joke is often on him. Chan first gained attention for his work in films like *Drunken Master* (1978), and he later reached superstar status in Hollywood when he was paired with Chris Tucker in the highly profitable *Rush Hour* franchise that began in the late '90s.

Another strong indication of Bruce Lee's influence on contemporary culture is the Wu-Tang Clan, the Staten Island hip hop collective that merged Asian martial arts with hip hop culture in creating one of the most original cultural statements in modern times. The Wu was led by RZA, who produced the music for Quentin Tarantino's film *Kill Bill* (2003). RZA presided over a group that included nine members, with several affiliates. The Wu called their home turf of Staten Island *Shaolin*, which is drawn from the landscape of the Shaw brothers' films and, in particular, a film called *The 36th Chamber of Shaolin* (1978), which also provided the name for one of the group members, Masta Killa. Throughout the '90s, the Wu-Tang Clan dropped classic hip hop tracks like "Cash Rules Everything Around Me

(C.R.E.A.M.)," "Can It Be All So Simple," and "Triumph," among many others. The members of the group all had solo careers as well, and made their presence known for both the collective work of the group and as individual artists.

Finally, Quentin Tarantino's film *Kill Bill* is a virtual homage to Bruce Lee and the interest in martial arts culture that Bruce's presence started back in the '70s. The film's main character, the Bride, played by Uma Thurman, wears a yellow tracksuit and the yellow-and-black Asics Tiger sneakers in the film, which is a direct link back to Bruce's outfit in *Game of Death*. The pagoda in *Game of Death* is also represented in the architecture of the final fight scene in *Kill Bill*, in which the central placement of the staircase is just like that of the staircase that Bruce must ascend on his way to the historic battle with Kareem. The Tarantino film also pays homage to other '70s martial arts films, particularly those of Run Run Shaw and his brother, Runme Shaw. Their famous Shaw Studios churned out many classic films that made their way to America, bad audio dubs and all; these would include films like *The Five Deadly Venoms* (1978), for instance.

RUDY RAY MOORE

In the early '70s, I was one of the first cats in my 'hood to get a portable cassette tape player/recorder. Quick to put my new technology to work, I went about the neighborhood trying to record anything I could find. I passed the mic around to my friends and other cats, who all said something, most of which amounted to

nothing, but it worked for what I was trying to accomplish. There was this one cat, though, a particularly inarticulate cat, if I can be completely honest, who said something that would transform my world.

Dude took the mic and began quoting from the vast catalog of Rudy Ray Moore, and my curiosity was forever piqued. Though dude was mad inarticulate otherwise, you would have thought that he had a Harvard Ph.D. in diction based on the way he flawlessly quoted the words of the man otherwise known as Dolemite. I was hooked, and after that I would do anything I could to get my hands on some Dolemite recordings.

For those of you who don't know, Rudy Ray Moore was a former singer who became a comic, but eventually came to be known for his long X-rated spoken-word soliloquies, which originally appeared on comedy albums that were called "blue records," then on cassette, and some of these routines have even made it onto CDs. Rudy Ray was a master of the toast, the practice of which some might also call signifyin'. Toasts and signifyin' are deeply rooted in the Black oral tradition. The practitioners of this art form are celebrated for their ability to spin a sexually explicit tale in a most creative and original fashion. One of the classics of this genre would have to be "The Signifying Monkey." This classic toast often changes with the teller, but Rudy Ray's version stands out for his original storytelling skills and his ability to make the piece his own statement.

As you might have already figured out, these practices are very much in line with what hip hop culture would become, and to this end, Rudy Ray Moore is one of the most sampled people in the history of hip hop. But before going there, it's important to point out that Rudy Ray made his name on the chitlin circuit, which referred to a loose consortium of Black theaters spread throughout many of the nation's urban areas. Comedy on the chitlin circuit was quite different from that normally associated with mainstream White comedy clubs, and especially different from what was allowed on television. For this reason, Rudy Ray had a huge Black underground following in the Super Fly '70s, but virtually no name recognition at all among White audiences.

While "The Signifying Monkey" demonstrates Rudy Ray Moore at work, this piece was relatively tame compared to some of his other recordings. There is "Dangerous Dan," "The Player," "Hurricane Annie," and, of course, "Petey Wheatstraw, The Devil's Son-in-Law," among countless other examples. In each of these, Rudy Ray brings a preacher's energy and articulation to these hilariously bawdy tales of his sexual exploits that are as compelling for his ability to rhyme as they are for the extremely un-PC nature of the toasts themselves. One of Moore's famous lines is "I've got a big black dick and it's good for lickin'/it'll make an ass out of Kentucky Fried Chicken." And this is just the tip of the Iceberg Slim here. Moore was crass, vulgar, offensive, and absolutely brilliant in the process. Many of his greatest routines remain on album and cassette, but you can hear some of his material on the CDs *Rudy Ray Moore Greatest Hits* (1995) and *Rudy Ray Moore—Raw, Rude & Real: More Greatest Hits* (2001).

Rudy Ray Moore was an underground sensation, and many hip hop artists have found inspiration in his words over the years. For instance, in hip hop, the exaggerated pronunciation of the word *bitch*, which is often pronounced *bi-at-ch!* originated with Rudy Ray Moore, was revived by Too Short in the '80s, and eventually came to be associated with Snoop Dogg, whose repeated use of this pronunciation would make it famous.

In the mid-'70s, at the height of the blaxploitation era, Rudy Ray Moore took his famous character to the big screen when he starred in *Dolemite* (1975). The film revolves around the life of Dolemite, a pimp who is released from prison in order to assist in capturing a thug named Willie Green, played by the film's director, D'Urville Martin. *Dolemite* is a low-budget classic that allows you to revel in the jump cuts, bad audio dubs, poor lighting, and countless appearances of the boom mic in the shot. The script is beyond terrible, but nonetheless it is hilarious that the film's star lists himself as screenwriter R. R. Moore in the credits. This is a feeble attempt to make it seem as though someone else actually wrote a movie for which there appears to be no real script in the first place.

Dolemite actually manages to get long sequences of his stage material in the film too, so you get to see him do his thing, no matter how ridiculous and unmotivated it seems relative to the rest of the film. Some of the other notable characters in the film include Lady Reed as Queen Bee, who serves as Dolemite's bottom woman who handles his hoes, and the infamous Hamburger Pimp, a junkie who gives Dolemite the word on the street while constantly hustling for hamburgers.

By the time Dolemite came out in the mid-'70s, blaxploitation had itself gotten to be much more high-end than it had been when it first started. As the genre got to be more successful, budgets went up and the movies over time tended to become more and more mainstream. But *Dolemite* was a throwback to the original days of the genre, with no pretension about being socially conscious or even remotely politically correct.

What makes the film so funny to me is the way that Rudy Ray Moore carries himself as an actor. Unlike Ron O'Neal, Max Julien, or Richard Roundtree, who were considered sex symbols in their films, Rudy Ray was no one's sex symbol, and he seemed not to give a fuck either. He was more like that famous Biggie Smalls line: "Heartthrob never/Black and ugly as ever," in no uncertain terms. There are several scenes in the film where he takes off his clothes for a sex scene, only to reveal his less-than-chiseled body. He is supposed to be a real fuckin' machine, though, and we are supposed to accept the fact that he has game and is irresistible to women. This is so funny because he is so earnest and such a bad actor. But all of this works quite well in the film, because everything about it is so bad that, in a roundabout way, the film turns out to be good. He is also supposed to be believable as an ass kicker who knows karate, as the film had to have the obligatory martial arts scene in it.

The movie *Dolemite* was so successful with its all-Black audiences that Rudy Ray went on to release *The Human Tornado* (1976), *Petey Wheatstraw* (1977), and *Disco Godfather* (1980), and in the process he left behind an important body of work. In these films, Rudy Ray's performances are actually captured and reproduced so that future generations will have evidence that something like this ever existed.

THE SPOOK WHO SAT BY THE DOOR (1973)
@

Director: Ivan Dixon
Studio: United Artists

The Super Fly '70s has gained a great deal of its street cred from films about pimps, players, and hustlers, but it is a political joint that remains the most intriguing film of the era. *The Spook Who Sat by the Door* is Ivan Dixon's film adaptation of Sam Greenlee's 1966 book by the same name, and it is nothing less than a cinematic classic.

For years, *The Spook* was the source of much urban legend, as the film was supposedly "lost" by United Artists studio. Other theories have suggested that the film—originally thought to be simply another "mindless" blaxploitation genre picture, like most of the other films of that era—was suppressed by the FBI because of its volatile political content. The only way to see the film was via bootlegged video copy. In 2003, the film was released on DVD for the first time, thanks to the efforts of actor Tim Reid, known primarily for his work on television's *WKRP in Cincinnati* and *Frank's Place*.

Interestingly enough, the film enters a culture now with somewhat different implications than was the case originally. *The Spook* by today's wisdom might be considered a film that promotes terrorism, depending on one's point of view. Some might see parallels between *The Spook* and Gillo Pontecorvo's classic *The Battle of Algiers* (1965). Set in the early '70s, though, the film "the spook who sat by the door"

The controversial best selling novel
now becomes a shocking screen reality.

BOKARI LTD. presents "THE SPOOK WHO SAT BY THE DOOR"
with LAWRENCE COOK · PAULA KELLY · JANET LEAGUE · J.A. PRESTON
Screenplay by SAM GREENLEE and MELVIN CLAY Based on the novel "THE SPOOK WHO SAT BY THE DOOR" by SAM GREENLEE
Produced by IVAN DIXON and SAM GREENLEE Associate Producer THOMAS G. NEUSOM Directed by IVAN DIXON
Music by HERBIE HANCOCK

PG

United Artists

73/292

"THE SPOOK WHO SAT BY THE DOOR"

seemed to incite fear based on its representation of a group of Black militants who have a plan to take over many of America's major cities by force in a political coup.

The Spook demonstrates the revolution that many Black nationalist groups like the Black Panther party often talked about during the 1960s and 1970s. The Panthers and other radical Black groups were also targets of the FBI's infamous COINTELPRO operation that sought to undermine their revolutionary attempts by any means necessary. It is for reasons such as this that the theory of the FBI's suppressing this controversial film has had so much credence in certain sections of the Black community.

The Spook deals with the CIA and its supposed attempts at integrating the agency. They are not really interested in integrating, but they stage a fixed competition to appease their opportunistic critics. When one Black man manages to slip under the radar and actually make the cut, all the fun begins.

Dan Freeman, known throughout the film simply as Freeman (Free-man), initially plays the role of the compliant sycophant— in other words, a handkerchief-head Uncle Tom. He eventually gains the trust of the CIA's brass, who assign him to menial duties in the third-floor basement, only to trot him out like a show horse when they want to demonstrate to visitors how progressive they are.

Freeman, played by actor Lawrence Cook, is slicker than he appears. He takes everything in, learns every lesson that the CIA has to teach, and finally quits his job to return to his hometown of Chicago. Once back in the Windy City, Freeman hooks up with the Cobras, a street gang, and goes about teaching them all that he has learned from the CIA. After the cops kill another

Black man in the 'hood, the now revolutionary Cobras take all of their CIA training and stage an insurgent revolution on the city. They take to the streets, to the airwaves, and anything else they can get their hands on as they bring the city to its knees. The film ends with Freeman toasting the revolution and preparing to take more cities across the country.

The term *spook* is a play on words. *Spook* is the CIA name used to identify spies, but it is also a twist on the derogatory implications of *spook* as a diss toward dark-skinned Black people. A *spook* in the negative sense derives from a name used to describe someone so black that they are virtually invisible, like a ghost. Freeman is both. He is a spy, but he is also a "spook"—someone who plays the stereotypical role of being in agreement with his White superiors, but who in actuality is plotting against them. As Freeman explains to the Cobras, stereotypes can work in their favor: "A Black man with a mop, broom, or tray can go anywhere in this country. A smiling Black man is invisible." Freeman also instructs them to be invisible and lie low, as it were: "If you sleep on the floor, you can't fall out of bed."

The message that many have taken from this film is that there is something strategic to being able to lie low and play the role, while having bigger plans in mind. It's about using people's stereotypes of you in your own favor by deceptively playing on their ignorance. *The Spook* is a lesson on life and how to live it in a racially imbalanced society in which image is often everything.

The film was directed by Ivan Dixon, best known for his acting work on the television show *Hogan's Heroes* (1965–71). Dixon also starred in films like the underrated *Nothing but a Man* (1964), and as the wise old sage who advises Bill Duke's wayward

Abdullah character in *Car Wash*. Dixon also directed a number of episodes of the popular television series *Magnum, P.I.* in the '80s.

The writer and producer Greenlee describes the film, which was shot in Chicago for a low budget and without permits, as "guerrilla cinema." He also claims in an interview that accompanies the DVD documentary that two brothers, Thomas and Dan Neusom, raised the money for the film from Black investors, with United Artists providing some completion funds.

The score for the film was provided by the great jazz artist Herbie Hancock.

COOLEY HIGH (1975)

Director: Michael Schultz
Studio: American International Pictures/MGM DVD

The overwhelming majority of films associated with the Super Fly '70s are truly representative of what had become the blaxploitation formula. These were films that in nearly every case revolved around crime, violence, sex, some articulation of Black power politics, and the conflicts with a corrupt White political establishment. But the era also featured Black family dramas like *Sounder* with Cicely Tyson, and comedies such as *Claudine*, starring Diahann Carroll and James Earl Jones, which dealt with the welfare system and its impact on poor Black families. *Sparkle* was an inspirational story about the trials and tribulations of a young Black woman's (Irene Cara) urban poverty and family dysfunction, and her rise to realizing her dreams of becoming a successful singer. *Car Wash* featured an ensemble cast that included Richard Pryor, the Pointer Sisters, Ivan Dixon, Bill Duke, veteran Black actor Clarence Muse, Antonio "Huggy Bear" Fargas, Franklin Ajaye, and Oakland Raiders football player Otis Sistrunk, among others, and was set around the humorous activities of a day in the life of several people working at an L.A. car wash.

I have never cared much for the "positive image" school of Black thought, so for this reason, the above-mentioned films are not suitable for inclusion in this guide because they were not properly urban and certainly not Super Fly. The film *Cooley High* is a notable exception, though. This film may not have fit into the blaxploitation formula, but it was most definitely urban, and most especially real in its representation of Black life in Chicago during the 1960s.

Cooley High, often referred to as the "Black *American Graffiti*" because of what some considered its similarity to that George Lucas film (1973), represented the life and times of Black screenwriter Eric Monte, whose experiences in high school and of growing up in the notorious Cabrini-Green housing projects of Chicago served as a basis for this coming-of-age urban tale. Monte, one of the few Black television writers of that time, had originally been a writer on *All in the Family*. He was later a writer and cocreator of *Good Times*. Monte was also the creator of the television show *What's Happening* (1976–79), which was loosely based on *Cooley High*. Monte represented the possibility that Black creative talent—who were not actors—could have an impact behind the camera in the creation of mainstream Black entertainment. But as the popularity of that Super Fly '70s Black moment faded, the possibilities of a critical mass of Black creative types in Hollywood faded as well.

In addition to Monte's creative presence, *Cooley High* was directed by another rising African American talent of the time, Michael Schultz, who directed *Car Wash* as well as the Richard Pryor star vehicles *Greased Lightning* (1977) and *Which Way Is Up?* Schultz looked poised to become one of the first Black crossover directors when he helmed *Sergeant Pepper's Lonely Hearts Club Band* (1978), but the film was both a commercial and critical failure, and Schultz's career never seemed to recover. Nonetheless, he was a momentary Black shining light in the '70s, and his success helped to pave the way for a new generation of Black filmmakers, like Spike Lee, Robert Townsend, and others who would begin their careers in the late 1980s.

Cooley High centers around the crazy antics of two high school friends: Preach, an aspiring writer and poet, played by Glynn Turman, and Cochise, a basketball player looking forward to going to Grambling College on an athletic scholarship, played by Lawrence Hilton-Jacobs. Turman has had a long career as a character actor, having appeared in other '70s films such as *Five on the Black Hand Side* (1973), *The River Niger* (1976), and *J.D.'s Revenge*, the latter of which was the basis for the remake *Bones*, starring Snoop Dogg. Turman may be best remembered now for his role as Colonel Brad Taylor on the sitcom *A Different World* (1987–93), and he often directed various episodes of the show also. From 1978 to 1984, Turman was married to the great Aretha Franklin, who sang the theme song for *A Different World*.

Lawrence Hilton-Jacobs had appeared in *Claudine* and *Roots* in the '70s, but became famous playing the suave jock Freddie "Boom Boom" Washington on the sitcom *Welcome Back, Kotter* (1975–79). He would later gain notoriety for his charged performance as patriarch Joe Jackson in the television miniseries *The Jacksons: An American Dream* (1992), about the dysfunctional inner workings of the famous Jackson entertainment clan.

Preach, Cochise, and their boy Pooter (Corin Rogers) engage in all manner of pranks, shenanigans, and bullshit while attending Cooley High. They skip school, chase girls, and shoot dice, among other things, all in the name of good fun, ghetto style. In the meantime, their cool but concerned teacher, Mr. Mason (played by Garrett Morris, the first Black cast member on *Saturday Night Live*), tries to pull their coats about life in the real world. All is fun and games until Preach and Cochise end up inadvertently hangin' out with some local thugs who just happen to be driving a stolen car. The casual pace of the film changes dramatically when Preach and Cochise find themselves on the run, trying to avoid the thugs, who assume that the fellas have snitched on them to the police. The film is great at mixing its overriding comedy with this dramatic turn of events.

A memorable scene from *Cooley High* showcases a classic Black house party, where a fight breaks out; this hilarious scene works to highlight the film's incredible Motown sound track. Some of the cuts on the sound track include "Baby Love" and "Stop, in the Name of Love" by Diana Ross and the Supremes; "I Can't Help Myself (Sugar Pie, Honey Bunch)" and "Reach Out, I'll Be There" by the Four Tops; "My Girl" by the Temptations; "Fingertips" by Stevie Wonder; and "Mickey's Monkey" by Smokey Robinson and the Miracles.

Yet in spite of all this musical star power, the song that had the biggest impact in the film was the G. C. Cameron ballad "It's So Hard to Say Goodbye to Yesterday." The relatively unknown Cameron had at one time been the lead singer of the Spinners and was also married to Gwen Gordy, who was the sister of Motown founder Barry Gordy. The gospel-tinged ballad closes the film quite strongly, and it would become a staple of Black high school graduation ceremonies for years to come. "It's So Hard to Say Goodbye" was eventually covered by the popular R & B group Boyz II Men on their 1991 multiplatinum-selling album *Cooleyhighharmony*, a title obviously inspired by the group's devotion to the film.

Cooley High has certainly served as an inspiration for modern-day Black filmmakers who have used the bonds of Black male friendship as the basis of their own stories, ranging from John Singleton's *Boyz n the Hood* (1991) to my nigga Rick Famuyiwa's *The Wood* (1991), a film where your man, the Notorious Ph.D., served as cowriter and producer.

The other example of *Cooley High*'s legacy comes in a scene where the fellas are drinking wine in the alley, while talking about their future. In the African tradition of pouring libations, or a liquid offering, Preach pours out a small amount of wine on the ground as a gesture of remembrance for the "brothas who ain't here." This sacred ritual of Black male culture is intended to show love to the brothas who are either dead or in jail. To this day, many Black men still engage in gestures of this kind as a way of demonstrating respect for their fallen homies. Examples of this can be heard on hip hop tracks like Ice Cube's "Dead Homiez"

(1990) and the Tupac song "Pour out a Little Liquor" from the soundtrack of *Above the Rim* (1994).

WATTSTAX (1973)

Director: Mel Stuart
Studio: Columbia Pictures/Warner Home Video

On August 20, 1972, the famed Stax record label out of Memphis hosted an all-day concert at the Los Angeles Coliseum to commemorate the seventh anniversary of the riots that took place in Watts, California. *Wattstax* is an effective documentation of the Super Fly '70s in all of its soulful, pimped-out ways. As part concert film and part documentary, *Wattstax* moves between performances by some of the label's leading artists, images of the abundant crowd, interviews with "real" Black people, an appearance by Jesse Jackson, and even several inserts of Richard Pryor narrating and providing commentary about Black life through his comedy.

To watch *Wattstax* is to transport yourself back to a fleeting moment of optimism in the early '70s, when social consciousness merged with regular folks gettin' their groove on. To observe the fashion and the dances, and to hear the joy and pain of everyone's own take on life at this most important moment is priceless, especially in an era when the realness of the culture often had to fight through the limited understanding of the Hollywood studio system in order to be heard. This film brought it to you from high, low, and everywhere else in between. *Wattstax* was, like the lyrics from the Dramatics song featured in the film, "Whatcha See Is Whatcha Get," "as real as real can get."

The film featured performances by many of the Stax label's top artists, including the Staple Singers, led by Roebuck "Pop" Staples and the amazing voice of his daughter Mavis; Rufus Thomas, wearing a pimped-out pink ensemble long before Cam'ron came on the scene; Johnnie Taylor; Luther Ingram; the Bar-Kays; and, of course, the biggest star on the label at the time, Isaac Hayes. Hayes, aka Black Moses, who closed the film, came out in his signature chains, as had become his custom at this time, after a rousing introduction by a young dashiki-wearing Jesse Jackson, who seemed innocent, determined, and quite charming, in contrast to what he would become years later.

Richard Pryor is hilarious as hell, as always, using bits from his routine to detail the intricacies of Black life in America, but from his deep-in-the-'hood perspective. One of the regular peo-ple who is featured in *Wattstax* happens to be Ted Lange, who got to be quite famous himself a few years after this as the fun-loving bartender Isaac on the television series *The Love Boat* (1977–86). Lange was definitely more militant with his comments in *Watt-stax* than anything he ever did on *The Love Boat*, which is why seeing him in the film is very funny, considering what he became.

CAR WASH (1976)

Director: Michael Schultz
Studio: Universal Pictures

By 1976, there were fewer and fewer films being made that directly and specifically addressed urban audiences. Increasingly, the films that were released had more of a crossover feel to them. *Car Wash* was a hilarious crossover romp that was centered around the activities of a crazy group of characters who come in contact with one another during a day in the life of an L.A. car wash. *Car Wash* was a film that relied on a mostly Black cast and a hip sound track featuring Norman Whitfield's group Rose Royce, but the film was quite different in its tone than many of the films released previously in the Super Fly '70s.

First of all, *Car Wash* was a comedy, and with the exception of films like Ossie Davis's *Cotton Comes to Harlem* (1970) and Oscar Williams's *Five on the Black Hand Side*, most of the films released during the blaxploitation era were action flix or dramas. There was always something funny going on in blaxploitation films, for sure. The characters in the films were trying so hard to be conscious of and in keeping with the politics of Black power, but consciousness was not thought to be humorous, so comedy was far from the intended genre—though depending on the film, laughter was often an appropriate response.

Yet with the release of Sidney Poitier's *Uptown Saturday Night* in 1974, with its all-star cast that included Poitier, Bill

Cosby, Richard Pryor, Flip Wilson, Rosalind Cash, Paula Kelly, Calvin Lockhart, Harry Belafonte, Roscoe Lee Brown, and the tap dancer Harold Nicholas of the famed Nicholas Brothers, among others, the Black urban comedy started to appear with increasing regularity, while the Black urban drama started to decline. This is an argument that could still be made today, as the remnants of that era live with us in contemporary Hollywood, where there remains a dearth of Black dramas, while Black comedies, many of them simply modern coon shows, continue to flourish. Poitier went on to direct two more "Black buddy" films in which he and Bill Cosby starred: *Let's Do It Again* and *A Piece of the Action*.

Clearly *Car Wash* was influenced by *Uptown Saturday Night's* ensemble casting approach. The film relied on several young actors, as well as some established names and a particular star whose cameo appearance is the funniest scene in the movie. Franklin Ajaye played Fly in *Car Wash*, a smooth-talkin' car wash employee with the oh, so perfect Afro who has his eye on Mona, a chick working at the greasy spoon across the street. Ajaye was a stand-up comic who over the years made several appearances on *The Tonight Show Starring Johnny Carson*, *The Late Show with David Letterman*, and on other programs like *Soul Train* as well. Ajaye was also a writer on *In Living Color*, *Roc*, and *NYPD Blue* in the 1990s.

Famous comedian George Carlin, one of the funniest men alive, plays a cabdriver in *Car Wash*. In 1972, Carlin released what many consider to be his best album, *Class Clown*, which contained the skit "Seven Words You Can Never Say on Television," which is his most famous work. He also was a regular on

The Tonight Show Starring Johnny Carson during this time, often serving as the guest host for the show when Carson was away.

Actor, writer, and director Bill Duke was just getting started in the '70s when he appeared in *Car Wash* as Duane, an angry young Muslim cat who insists on being called Abdullah. Duke was originally a writer on *Good Times* before going on to appear in films like *American Gigolo* (1980), *Commando* (1985), *The Predator* (1987), and *Menace II Society*. He began working as a television director on *Knots Landing* in 1979 and went on to direct other popular television shows like *Cagney and Lacey*, *Hill Street Blues*, and *Miami Vice*, as well as films like *A Rage in Harlem* (1991) and *Deep Cover* (1992). In *Car Wash*, Abdullah decides to rob the car wash after being sent home earlier in the day by the manager. It is only after a long talk with the elder statesman of the car wash, actor and director Ivan Dixon (who plays Lonnie in the film), that Abdullah reconsiders and opens up to Lonnie about his struggles in life. The film also stars the ubiquitous Antonio Fargas; this time, though, Fargas breaks away from the Huggy Bear stereotype to play Lindy, a flamboyantly gay car wash attendant.

The best scene in the film is a cameo appearance by Richard Pryor, who plays Daddy Rich, one pimped-out, bling-drippin' hustler of a preacher, who has a message of prosperity for all who will listen: "For a small fee, I'll set you free, nearer thy God to thee." Daddy Rich is accompanied by the Wilson Sisters, played by the Pointer Sisters, one of the female singing groups makin' much noise in the '70s. The versatile Pointer Sisters, who at the time dressed as though they were from the 1940s, had a top-twenty pop hit with the single "Yes, We Can Can" in 1973. In

1974, the Pointer Sisters released the single "Fairy Tale," a country-and-western song, which they performed at the famous Grand Ole Opry in Nashville, Tennessee, becoming the first Black female group ever to appear at that venue. They later went on to earn a Grammy Award for Best Country Performance by a Duo or Group in 1975 for that song. In 1975, they scored a number one R & B hit with "How Long (Betcha Got a Chick on the Side)." In *Car Wash*, they perform "You Gotta Believe"; it was one of the highlights of the sound track and was later sampled by Ice Cube on his hit "Really Doe" in 1993.

In this same scene veteran Black actor Clarence Muse appears as Snapper, the shoeshine man, who is a devout follower of Daddy Rich. Muse began acting in the silent era, and his body of work spans from the early 1920s to the late 1970s. He was never a star, and many of his appearances were not credited, but over the years he appeared in notable films like *Hearts in Dixie* (1929), *Huckleberry Finn* (1931), *Show Boat* (1936) with the great Paul Robeson, *Gone With the Wind* (1939), *Porgy and Bess* (1959), and the Sidney Poitier/Harry Belafonte film *Buck and the Preacher* (1972).

Car Wash was directed by Michael Schultz and was written by Joel Schumacher, who also wrote *Sparkle* and *The Wiz* (1978). Schumacher went on to become a noted Hollywood director with such films as *St. Elmo's Fire* (1985), *Cousins* (1989), *Batman Forever* (1995), *A Time to Kill* (1996), and *Phantom of the Opera* (2004).

Much of the film's sound track is performed by the Norman Whitfield–produced group Rose Royce, which featured the lead vocal talents of Gwen Dickey. The Rose Royce tracks work throughout the music-laden movie, and the success of these tracks started a run for the group for the next three years. The title track, *Car Wash*, was a number one pop single, and the album itself went platinum. "I Wanna Get Next to You" and "I'm Going Down," which would later be covered by Mary J. Blige, both became top-ten R & B singles as well. In 1977, the group released their next album, entitled *Rose Royce II: In Full Bloom*, scoring two more top-ten hits with "Do Your Dance" and "Ooh Boy," and the following year they hit the top five on the R & B charts with "I'm in Love" and the classic "Love Don't Live Here Anymore."

ACROSS 110TH STREET (1972)

Director: Barry Shear
Studio: United Artists

One of the truly underappreciated classic films of the era is Barry Shear's *Across 110th Street* (1972). Many people probably know a reference to this film only because they've heard the Bobby Womack theme song from the film used as the opening to Quentin Tarantino's homage to the blaxploitation era, *Jackie Brown*. But *Across 110th Street* stands on its own as an excellent example of the gritty urban crime joints that the early '70s came to be known for.

Harlem is the geographical destination to which one arrives as he crosses 110th Street in New York City. The film suggests early on that Harlem is contested territory, and, like many of the other films of the era, the movie is defined by a battle over this turf. When the film begins, two armed robbers, dressed as cops, burst in on the Mafia's "bank." This is where the Italian mobsters and their Black colleagues add up the proceeds from all their illegal affairs. The robbers shoot up the joint, kill all the gangsters, and take the loot. They run outside to the getaway car and end up killing two cops as they are escaping. This means that now the robbers have the Italian mob, Harlem's own Black gangsters, and the cops on their ass. This conflict sets the flick in motion, and it all turns into a battle over control for Harlem.

Many films of the era deal with the battle over ghetto turf that ensued when the ideas of Black nationalism started seeping into the underworld. In the films of this era Black gangsters, like Black radicals and others, felt that everything in the 'hood should be controlled by Black people—even criminal enterprise. Yet, up to a certain point, the Italian mob had pretty much controlled these rackets, and they were not so eager to abandon them either. The Mafia don in *Across 110th Street* says, in what has to be the worst Italian accent on film, "We cannot lose Harlem." He goes on to warn his capo that "They're rough, those niggers."

This scene indicates the racial tension at the heart of this debate over power in *Across 110th Street*, and this tension could also be seen in other gangster films from the era, like the all-time classic *The Godfather* (1972), which was the reigning gangster film of the '70s and for all time. In *The Godfather* there is the famous scene of the meeting of the heads of the five Mafia families, where one of the mobsters drops this racial bomb regarding drugs: "We leave the traffic to the dark people. The colored. They're animals anyway. Let them lose their souls." This scene had a lot of real-life implications in terms of the underworld, race, crime, and control of the lucrative drug trade, not to mention the role of the cops in policing and/or occupying the Black community as well. The conflict over power and control jumps off in relation to these societal issues, and this historical backdrop would have informed the mind-set of the people who saw *Across 110th Street* when it was in the theaters at that time.

The racial conflict is raw in this joint, and it's on all sides too. Both the gangsters and the cops are divided by race. Anthony Franciosa plays Nick D'Salvio, a hard-core gangster who has married the boss's daughter and is trying to work his way up to demonstrate to his father-in-law that he is fit to run things. Richard Ward, a veteran of many Black films over the years, including *Mandingo*, stars as the Black don, Doc Johnson. In one memorable scene, Doc calls D'Salvio out and labels him "the boss's errand boy." D'Salvio spouts off racist remarks on the regular and walks through the 'hood as though he truly doesn't give a fuck. He meets his death in a hail of machine gun fire near the end of the film.

Doc Johnson is also in conflict with an older racist cop named Matelli, played by Anthony Quinn. Matelli, we find out, has been on Doc's payroll for a long time, but he feels squeezed out by the arrival of a new Black cop named Pope, played by the venerable actor Yaphet Kotto, who is probably best known to contemporary fans for his work on the television show *Homicide* in the 1990s. In one of the best scenes in the film, Matelli attempts to confront Doc, only to be exposed as being on the take. Richard Ward had an incredibly unique voice that was both deep and quite hoarse, something like that of Miles Davis. At one point Doc yells to Matelli, "You watch your mouth, white boy. You might be something big to those booty butts that you work over down at the station, but this is me, Doc muthafuckin' Johnson!" This has to be one of the greatest disses in the history of cinema. That's classic, right there. To this end, I have often thought of myself as "Doc muthafuckin' Boyd" as well.

There is also a beef between Matelli and Pope, the two cops. This element of the story perhaps reflected the conflict over the government program known as affirmative action, which was being hotly debated during this time and continues to be a divisive issue today. Matelli, an older White cop, is being supplanted by the younger Pope, who is not only Black, but also has a college background. Their styles are different too. Matelli is an abusive cop in the mode of Clint Eastwood's Dirty Harry character, who berates, physically abuses, and violates the Miranda rights of Black suspects. Doc even refers to him as a "racist son of a bitch," a title that Matelli is none too quick to dismiss.

Pope, on the other hand, does everything by the book. He wants to gain Matelli's respect and wants Matelli to see him as an equal. Doc tries to exploit this tension and appeals to Pope by offering bribes and clues on the case. Pope is unfazed by all of this.

One of the more colorful characters in the film is, once again, Antonio Fargas, an icon of the era who later became famous on the television show *Starsky and Hutch* (1975–79). His character, Henry J., is one of the robbers who takes the loot at the beginning of the film. Unlike his partners, who are lyin' low, Henry J. is set to go out and party. He is intent on spending some of his newly acquired money in grand fashion. So he gets dressed, sprays on some Afro Sheen, one of the popular Black hair-care products of the day, and lights up a fat-ass joint. Henry J. is clean as the board of health when he steps out in his red derby, his multicolored suede jacket, and long scarf. This is the scene that he himself would parody some years later in *I'm Gonna Git You Sucka*. We later see Henry J. in the ho house with several hoes of many races: Black, White, and Asian. He is spending money, getting "highed up," as they say in the film, and definitely getting his freak on when D'Salvio and company bust into the spot. D'Salvio yells out, "Hey, nigger," to which Henry J. responds, "You talkin' to me, white man?" D'Salvio goes on to yank the coke spoon off Henry J.'s neck, smashes a glass in his face, and then proceeds to castrate him. Henry J. went out like a lame, but he was talkin' shit all the way.

The conclusion of *Across 110th Street* is, in many ways, indicative of what made the films from the blaxploitation era so successful. Even though all of the robbers get killed, there is still something affirming for urban audiences. While the last of the remaining robbers, the character Jim Harris, is getting shot repeatedly on the roof of a building, he throws the bag of money over to a crowd of eagerly awaiting children, who get to be the innocent beneficiaries of all that has gone down. These kids represent the people, and to this end, the film concludes on a strong Robin-in-the-'Hood note that worked well for the urban audiences who were checking this film out.

PART

3

If You Don't Know Me by Now

SOUL MUSIC, SOUL POWER

What the '70s flix did for the eyes, the music did for the ears, adding another important link to the Super Fly '70s chain. The music of the era provided the hip sounds that make this one of the most important musical decades ever, and like the flix, this music created a sound that will forever be associated with the '70s, but it still has strong resonance today.

Take, for example, the group behind the *Sweet Sweetback's Baadasssss Song* sound track, known back then as the Elements of the Universe. I am specifically referring to the group Earth Wind and Fire. EWF, who often invoked astrological imagery and elements of Egyptology on their album covers and in their music, would go on to make a name for themselves throughout the '70s with stellar albums like *That's the Way of the World* (1975), *Gratitude* (1975), and *All 'N All* (1977), among many others. The group joined forces with Ramsey Lewis on the classic *Sun Goddess*, which itself was a reuniting of Lewis and EWF leader Maurice White, who had been a member of Lewis's band at an earlier time.

I point out EWF and the *Sweetback* sound track here because not only were sound tracks an integral part of the success of the blaxploitation genre, but Black music in general was also an important part of the overall vibe of the '70s, serving as the soul of this incredible cultural movement.

Take for example, the merger of science fiction, Black cosmology, and unadulterated funk put forth by George Clinton and his interchangeable units Parliament and Funkadelic, often referred to as a combination of the two group names, Parliament Funkadelic, with the music they produced known as P. Funk, which was short for "pure funk." Clinton, a former hairdresser from New Jersey, had originally been signed to Motown Records, recording with his group under the name the Parliaments. Motown was trying to model Clinton's band in the image of the slick, well-dressed, choreographed style of the immensely successful group the Temptations.

Clinton eventually left the Motown label and soon began recording a series of records that seemed to have been highly influenced by the type of work that Jimi Hendrix was doing on the 1970 album *Band of Gypsies*. Clinton albums from the early '70s, like *Maggot Brain* and *Cosmic Slop*, are indicative of an attempt to reclaim rock and roll and return this music to its Black roots. But it wasn't until the mid-'70s that Clinton really seemed to find his sweet spot, when he began recording a series of albums and singles that would redefine Black dance music and make funk a style all unto itself. Some of these albums and singles include: *Up for the Down Stroke, Chocolate City, The Mothership Connection, Clones of Dr. Funkenstein, Funkentelechy vs. the Placebo Syndrome, Motor-Booty Affair, Tales of Kidd Funkadelic,*

Hardcore Jollies, One Nation Under a Groove, Uncle Jam Wants You, "P. Funk (Wants to Get Funked Up)," "Give up the Funk (Tear the Roof off the Sucker)," "Flashlight," "Aqua Boogie," and "(Not Just) Knee Deep." In 1976 alone the ever-elusive though highly productive Clinton delivered five albums, using four different group names, for three different record labels.

Much of Clinton's music during this time was a crazy avant-garde combination that merged images of science fiction with Black power rhetoric articulated as though one were on an extended acid trip. A great deal of Clinton's success was achieved through his association with the notorious disco mogul Neil Bogart and his Casablanca Records label. For Clinton's legendary live concerts, known as the "P. Funk Earth Tour," Bogart supported Clinton's vision and provided him access to the same set designers as those of the rock groups KISS and the Rolling Stones. Bogart's financial backing afforded Clinton the opportunity to have an elaborate stage show that functioned something like a funk opera. Here the mother ship would descend to Earth, and Clinton's main character, Dr. Funkenstein, would emerge, often having to do battle with his archnemesis, Sir Nose, who of course was "devoid of funk." In 1977 *Parliament Live: The P. Funk Earth Tour* was released as an album.

Clinton's elaborate tales often contained coded messages, sometimes channeling Black power ideology through metaphors like that of "Chocolate City," a reference to the increasing number of urban cities such as Detroit and Washington, DC, with large Black populations and newly elected Black officials. On other occasions the message might not be political, but it was always funny, like that of the single "Aqua Boogie," in which the lyrics cleverly alluded to an aversion to performing cunnilingus.

Clinton was very much a representative of the second half of the '70s, where a strong sense of hedonism, debauchery, and freedom of expression seemed to be taking the place of the earnest, strident political leanings of the earlier part of the decade. This coincides with the emergence of the disco culture and all its attendant indulgences of sex and drugs. The look of Clinton's fifty-plus-member band fit right in with the times, as there was a range of wild shit going on, from Clinton's own crazy hairstyles to cats in diapers to other cats in wedding dresses, long before Dennis Rodman was even heard of. This vibe of the funky Black acid trip was, unlike Hendrix's music, targeted specifically at urban Black audiences. The music and the imagery were groundbreaking, as was the overall experience itself. Clinton had become an institution, spinning off several different units of the whole P. Funk experience and creating what amounted to a P. Funk nation, all operating under the same groove.

George Clinton and his music were also very influential on hip hop, starting in the late '80s, when producers began moving away from their reliance on James Brown samples and started to raid the storehouse of all Clinton's classic beats. The person most responsible for reworking the Clinton sound in hip hop and using it as a new blueprint for the music is Dr. Dre. His work, originally with N.W.A. (Niggaz With Attitude), but most important on his own groundbreaking album *The Chronic*—which is basically a tribute to Clinton's classic *Mothership Connection*—and in his collabo with Snoop Dogg on his first solo album, *Doggy Style*, made the funk sound good all over again, but this time with superb gangsta lyrics and the laid-back style of Snoop to go over the top of those funky-ass beats. In the video from *The Chronic's* single "Let Me Ride," old footage from a *Mothership Connection* concert tour is used.

Dre was not the only hip hop producer to use samples from Clinton's previous work, though. The P. Funk catalog became like the bible for hip hop sounds for a period of time when most every producer sampled something that Clinton had already created to enhance their own contemporary musical expression. Notable among this group were producers like Erick Sermon and his work with EPMD (Erick and Parrish Makin' Dollars), as well as the group Digital Underground. To me, the loose though collective energy created by the whole P. Funk enterprise was also influential on the hip hop collective Wu-Tang Clan, who used the imagery of martial arts culture and kung fu cinema the way Clinton had used science fiction in merging an Asian aesthetic with a hard-core street sensibility, in turn creating one of the most original statements ever made in hip hop history.

So, with all that, let's move on to some of the shining lights of music that defined the Super Fly '70s. I continue with the gentlemen I refer to as "the Three Kings": Marvin Gaye, Curtis Mayfield, and Stevie Wonder. I'll spend some time discussing their collective impact before moving on to highlight some of their signature works. Then there is the Queen of Soul herself, my homey, Miss Aretha Franklin. Having dealt with the kings and queens, we move on to the godfather; that's the Godfather of Soul, James Brown. And then onto "the Dude" himself, Quincy Jones. After that, I deal with my man Jimi Hendrix, who was always on some other shit, especially on his album *A Band of Gyp-*

sies. Following Hendrix is a list of artists who stand out for their own unique contributions to the times: Rick James, Barry White, Herbie Hancock, Al Green, the Isley Brothers, the Ohio Players, and that conscientious brotha Gil Scott-Heron. After which I focus on the ubiquitous Philadelphia International record label, before spittin' some game about two of my favorite singles, William DeVaughn's "Be Thankful for What You Got" and the Undisputed Truth's "Smiling Faces Sometimes."

THREE KINGS

If there were a Mount Rushmore of the Super Fly '70s, the figures represented would have to be Marvin Gaye, Curtis Mayfield, and Stevie Wonder. Each artist in his own way helped to usher in the era of the singer/songwriter/producer—and this meant that what you heard reflected the musical vision of the individuals and not simply the commercial interests of the record company.

In the case of Marvin and Stevie, their break from the Motown tradition helped to take that label in another direction. In the '60s, the Motown sound reached the masses with its assembly-line style of production under the watchful eye of label founder and Black music pioneer Barry Gordy. Yet by the '70s, as Black people throughout America went about transforming their identity, Motown's signature style was starting to sound prepackaged and was becoming repetitive. Both Marvin and Stevie, after a protracted struggle with Gordy, were successful in gaining their independence, and in so doing were able to create music that defined the times and came to be the template for a future generation of singers, rappers, and producers.

Curtis Mayfield started his own independent label, Curtom. This, too, was a practice that would inspire many modern-day hip hop figures, like Russell Simmons, Diddy, and Eazy-E, among many others, in which an independent spirit and sense of ownership define the ways they do business.

What Marvin, Curtis, and Stevie did was use the musical format as a way to articulate their own personal politics, which were set against the backdrop of what was going on in the streets of Black America at the time. They often combined the personal, the political, and the spiritual in really impressive ways to highlight their individuality, while reflecting on the overall condition of Black people, and by extension the nation at large. These artists found a way to let their voices be heard, and the artistry that they recorded will forever be indicative of one of the best eras ever in the history of Black music.

MARVIN GAYE, *WHAT'S GOING ON?* (1971)

There is no musical figure whose work better represents the Super Fly '70s to me than the late, great Marvin Gaye. Though Gaye was a native of Washington, DC, it was in the city of my birth, Detroit, that he gained fame and fortune as the star of the venerated Motown label. When you consider the luminous roster of

Motown, with artists like Stevie Wonder, the Temptations, and Smokey Robinson, this was no small feat.

Motown in the '60s had become what its founder, Barry Gordy, often described as "Hitsville, USA," drawing liberally on the symbolism of Detroit's very existence by invoking the assembly-line metaphor made famous by the auto industry. Gordy produced hit after hit in the '60s as his assembly-line approach made Black music palatable for mainstream American society. With the same precision that General Motors used to produce cars, Gordy produced hit records that came to serve as the sound track for a great deal of America during that important and transitional time in the nation's history that focused on race.

In many ways, though, Detroit's auto industry in the '60s was on its last leg. In an era before high gas prices and Japanese import cars, the American auto industry had the game on lock and faced no competition for its throne. Gordy, for a time, was the only game in town when it came to an independently Black-owned record label. His success was such that he became a role model for future generations in that he ran a successful Black-owned music label in an industry where many great Black performers were merely hired stagehands. In the same way, Gordy's success, like that of the American auto industry, began to cloud his vision. He was so adept at making hits that he lost touch with the streets, and this is where Marvin Gaye's *What's Going On?* comes into play.

When Gaye first approached his label head and brother-in-law Gordy about doing an album that reflected the reality of life in the late '60s, Gordy was opposed. Marvin Gaye was deeply affected by the civil rights movement and the anti–Vietnam War movement, and he wanted to deal in his music with all the societal upheaval that was ravaging the nation. Yet Gordy wanted Marvin to continue recording pop songs like "Hitch Hike" (1962) and "I Heard It Through the Grapevine" (1968), songs that had done quite well for Motown. Marvin had also recorded several duet albums with female artists like Tammi Terrell, Kim Weston, and the emerging star Diana Ross.

Marvin's work with Terrell stands out. Some of their more popular songs were "Ain't No Mountain High Enough" and "You're All I Need to Get By." In 1967, Terrell collapsed in Marvin's arms while performing onstage, which may have been the beginning of her slow decline as the effects of a brain tumor began to take their toll on her health. She eventually died in 1970. Marvin was so distraught that he was unable to perform or record for several years afterward. Urban legend has often suggested that Terrell's tumor was the result of the regular beat-downs she received from her lover, Motown singer David Ruffin. Terrell was also once linked romantically to James Brown.

By the early '70s, Marvin was becoming increasingly concerned with breaking out of the Motown formula. He wanted to get off the assembly line and make records that were focused and more introspective. Marvin really wanted to express himself and do something that was both personal and political. He achieved all of this and then some with the release of the album *What's Going On?* (1971), in which he performed, wrote, and produced most of the songs.

Gordy, who felt that the album was too political and wouldn't sell, originally refused to release the album. In addition, Gordy had previously insisted that his talent keep the producing, song-writing, and performing chores separate, but Marvin blurred all of that. His deep involvement in all aspects of the record allowed the expression of Marvin's true artistry to shine through.

What's Going On?, the album, is anchored by three strong singles, all of which reached number one on the charts: the title track, "What's Going On?," "Mercy Mercy Me (The Ecology)," and "Inner City Blues (Makes Me Wanna Holler)." While each of these singles was phenomenal in its own right, it is the entirety of the album that makes it such a profound musical statement. As a matter of fact, I would advise listening to the album in one sit-ting so you get the full vibe that Marvin intended.

What's Going On? came to be known as a concept album, which was a popular style and trend in the music industry of the '70s. A concept album is conceived as a whole, and all of the songs on the album contribute to an overall theme and effect a unified mood. The record business at the time was intent on getting singles out of albums for radio play, but in the case of the concept album, it was the entire album that merited one's attention. Concept albums were not something that soul singers had been identified with before *What's Going On?* Yet other peo-ple, like Stevie Wonder, Marvin's Motown label mate, and Cur-tis Mayfield, two of the other stellar artists of the time period, would, over time, also come to be known for their own concept albums.

In the case of *What's Going On?*, Marvin's concept had to do with riffing on the ills of contemporary American society regarding Vietnam, the plight of urban America, the environment, political corruption, drug addiction, and spirituality, these topics being the key issues in understanding the problems of the larger world. Marvin captured a mood and expanded on the sentiment. The album was highly personal, while at the same time very political and of the moment.

The single "What's Going On?" is one of the most popular songs released in the '70s of any genre in sales and overall recognition. It has become an anthem of the time, the counterculture, and the anti–Vietnam War movement, and it is continually used to represent the 1970s for contemporary audiences in all forms of media. Though it's hard for me to embrace something that is so popular, this is one of those rare cases where popularity and critical acclaim come together.

During his brief, self-imposed exile from the music game from 1970 to 1972, while he mourned the death of his colleague Tammi Terrell, Marvin decided to try his hand at another game by stepping on the gridiron. He had a tryout with the Detroit Lions in 1970, and though he did not make the team, he remained friends with players like Lem Barney and Mel Farr, whose voices can be heard talkin' shit at the beginning of the song "What's Going On?" Marvin also spent time training to be a pugilist as well, but he eventually found his way back to the recording studio and the stage after staying away for almost two years.

On "What's Going On?," Marvin dropped many lines that

would become classic in the realm of music. He said, "War is not the answer/'cause only love can conquer hate," for instance, and this line has been used repeatedly since that time whenever it appeared an unpopular war was brewing—even as recently as 2003, when George W. Bush was about to invade Iraq. Marvin's lyrics about the waste of war and the resulting attitudes around it created a statement on peace that has seldom, if ever, been offered in such a concise musical form.

On "What's Happening Brother?," the second song on the album, Marvin is singing about a conversation he had with his brother Frankie, who had recently returned from Vietnam. Though the title refers to Marvin's blood brother, it could have very easily been referring to the notion of a "brotha," the common term used to refer to other Black men in general, as the ideas of the times suggested that all Black men were indeed brothers. The title could be interpreted directly, as in Marvin asking his own brother, or it could be thought of as a question about the condition of the Black man in America. It works either way and speaks to the universality of Marvin's vision, in that it is general as well as specific. The rhetorical question, "What's happening?" came to be a common greeting among many brothas as well.

The third song is "Flyin' High (In the Friendly Sky)," which has to do with drug use or "gettin' high," one of Marvin's favorite pastimes. The use of a popular airline metaphor was all about explaining the feeling of an altered state. Marvin talked about flying high "without ever leaving the ground." The explanation of his addiction was a haunting personal journey into the dark reaches of his mind. He speaks about going to the place where "danger awaits me." He admits that "self-destruction is in my hand" and declares himself "crazy" when he can't find what he's in need of. The coldest—and perhaps most poetic—line in the whole song is when Marvin sings about "the boy who makes slaves out of men," a reference to the street name for heroin. Heroin was often called *boy* or in some cases, *the gentleman*, while cocaine was referred to as *girl*.

So in the first three tracks, Marvin has gone from the overtly political to the inherently personal, yet on the fourth track he switches it up again. This time he begins to call on his roots in the Black church when he does "Save the Children," which then segues into "God Is Love." What is so striking about his "Save the Children" is the way that Marvin overdubs his own voice, so that he is doing both the call and the response.

The sixth track and one of the greatest singles off the album, "Mercy, Mercy Me" ("things ain't what they used to be") is so important because it is one of the first songs and one of the few soul songs ever to deal with environmental issues, long before these issues were thought of as significant political issues (as is the case now). Marvin's comments about overpopulation, nuclear radiation, and "fish full of mercury," among other things, were so important, yet so absent from discussions in Black popular culture at the time, when people were so intensely focused on the issue of race. Marvin was a visionary when you consider the role that the discussion of the environment plays in today's society.

The track "Wholy Holy" again takes Marvin back to his religious roots. Marvin's father was a minister in Washington, DC, and their relationship was always a difficult one. It is assumed that Marvin's choice to sing secular music created a further rift in their relationship due to his father's overt religious fundamentalism. However, Marvin never completely abandoned the church in his sound or in his lyrics. He was often fusing the sacred and the secular in really interesting ways, and "Wholy Holy" is but one example of this in his music.

The great Aretha Franklin, another minister's child, covered "Wholy Holy" on her groundbreaking live gospel album, *Amazing Grace*, in 1972. Aretha appears on the album cover dressed to the hilt in a fly African cultural style, head wrap and all, barefoot down. The record itself is nothing short of amazing, even for a nonreligious muthafucka like myself. Her version of "Wholy Holy," though quite different from Marvin's original version, is on point nonetheless.

Finally, *What's Going On?* concludes with "Inner City Blues." This is Marvin's ode to urban poverty, a street anthem in which he declares that the conditions of the inner city are such that they "make me wanna holla" and "throw up both my hands." His mention of "trigger-happy policing" points to the inner city and the antagonism that has long typified the relationship between the cops and members of the Black community. Years later Grand-Master Flash and the Furious Five featuring Melle Mel would again discuss the problem of the urban underclass in "The Message," one of the most important hip hop tracks ever recorded, and a descendant of Marvin's "Inner City Blues."

What's Going On? was really an exception in Marvin's overall career. He is much more well-known for sexual songs, like "Let's Get It On" (1973), which reached number one on both the pop and R & B charts; "I Want You" (1976), also a number one R & B hit; and his last number one hit on the Motown label, the dance track "Got to Give It Up" (1977). The live version of

"Distant Lover" is also an all-time fan favorite (1974). Marvin scored a huge hit with the single "Sexual Healing," which appeared on the album *Midnight Love* (1982). This album, released by the Columbia label, was his first album on a label other than Motown. "Sexual Healing" became a number one hit and won two Grammy Awards in 1983, while the *Midnight Love* album achieved platinum status.

Some of the more interesting material in his musical catalog can be found in *Here, My Dear* (1978), a late Motown album that he recorded to help pay some of the spousal support he owed to his wife, Anna Gordy, Barry's sister. Marvin was so personal on this album about his failed marriage to Anna, a much older woman, that she is reported to have thought about suing him for invasion of privacy.

One of my personal favorites is the next album after *What's Going On?*, the sound track to the film *Trouble Man* (1972). The single "Trouble Man" is one of the best singles of the entire era. The album itself features some of the coolest instrumentals of the period and still resonates as a source of break beats for hip hop producers today.

I would also point out an album called *Vulnerable*, which was a series of standards that Marvin originally recorded in 1967 and continued to tweak throughout the '70s, though the album was released only posthumously by Motown in 1997. This album featured Marvin and jazz composer Bobby Scott doing what was in essence an album of jazz standards. Marvin was never satisfied in his lifetime with the recording, but it remains an excellent example of his versatility as an artist in spite of certain limitations.

Marvin's latter years were marked by a serious decline due to his excessive drug use. He did experience some triumphs, though, before being tragically shot and killed by his own father in 1984. He made a brief comeback in the early '80s with the megahit "Sexual Healing," and then he sang the best rendition of the national anthem ever when he performed at the 1983 NBA All-Star Game in Los Angeles.

Marvin's work obviously influences a number of today's singers, notably someone like Maxwell, though Marvin's impact could be heard across a broad spectrum of contemporary artists. In hip hop, Dr. Dre made good use of "Inner City Blues" as a sample for his work on the D.O.C.'s track "The Formula," but the best use of Marvin's music and voice to date would have to be Erick Sermon's sampling of Marvin's "Turn on Some Music" (1982) to create a new song called "Music" in 2001.

CURTIS MAYFIELD,
SUPER FLY (1972)

Curtis Mayfield has to be one of the most underrated musical artists ever. He doesn't enjoy the immediate name recognition that contemporaries Marvin Gaye and Stevie Wonder have enjoyed over the years, but his musical output was just as important to the time period. From his early work with the Impressions to his incredible production work on several blaxploitation sound tracks in the '70s, Curtis was a talented singer, guitarist, composer, and producer who helped define the overall consciousness of the era.

Many people, for instance, remain unaware of the tragedy

that Curtis encountered in 1990. While performing outdoors in Brooklyn during inclement weather, stage lighting equipment fell on him, paralyzing him from the neck down. Though he continued to try to record, he died unceremoniously in 1999.

The Chi-town native spanned the spectrum of Black consciousness, though, from originally being closely aligned with the music of the Black church and the civil rights movement in the 1960s, to the more militant Black power rhetoric that came to define his music in the 1970s. He went from reworking an old gospel standard, "Amen," in the '60s, to the song "Kung Fu" in the mid-'70s, which features the poignant opening line "My mother borned me in the ghetto/there was no mattress for my head." He goes on to say that in spite of the similarities surrounding the conditions of their birth, his mother would not name him Jesus because, "I wasn't white enough, she said."

Curtis is best known, however, for the sound track for the 1972 film *Super Fly*.

I will spend significant time dealing with the sound track later, but this may be a good opportunity to trace some of the steps that led up to this monumental musical achievement. In the mid-'60s, Curtis Mayfield and the Impressions began releasing a string of hits that directly connected to the politics expressed during the civil rights movement. With "Keep on

Pushing" and "People Get Ready" you can still hear the gospel influence in the music, as it speaks metaphorically to the coming changes in society that Curtis associates with Dr. Martin Luther King Jr. and the politics of the day.

Yet on tunes like "Choice of Colors" and "We People Who Are Darker Than Blue" (one of the greatest titles in the history of music), the lyrics, though still civil rights oriented, starts to become more direct in its address. His single "We're a Winner" became an anthem of sorts for the civil rights movement and was even banned on some radio stations as being too militant. He exclaims that "we're moving on up" in terms of the progress of the movement's efforts, while also providing a future hook to the famous theme song to the '70s sitcom *The Jeffersons* as performed by Ja'Net DuBois, who was better-known as the character Willona from *Good Times*.

In the early '70s, Curtis left the Impressions to pursue a solo career as well as start his own record label, Curtom Records. One of the early releases on the Curtom label was Curtis's incredible 1971 live performance from New York's Bitter End nightclub, simply entitled *Curtis/Live! Live!* is such a strong record because he's starting to move in a more militant direction politically.

Curtis/Live! begins with the song "Mighty Mighty (Spade and Whitey)," which, in a racially provocative way, spells out his ironically biting, cynical approach to the state of race relations. This sentiment began to color much of Curtis's music at this point in his career. This song also stands out because of the break section in the song, when Curtis sings "we don't need no music/we got soul," killing everything in the band except for the ample percussion sound. This presages the club chant, "The roof is on fire/we don't need no water/let the muthafucka burn/burn muthafucka burn," that has long been a part of the urban dance scene. Similar in theme to "Mighty, Mighty" is another track on the album entitled "(Don't Worry) If There's a Hell Below We're All Going to Go." This track would become quite well-known for Curtis's exaggerated enunciation of a string of racial epithets before the song actually begins: "Niggers, Jews, Whiteys." He also calls out "police and their backers," signaling Richard Nixon's campaign for law and order, which many interpreted as a call for police brutality to slow the political violence that had become commonplace in the 'hood at this time. Curtis even chastises Nixon by name in the live performance of the song.

The last song on *Curtis/Live!*, "Stone Junkie," really sets the table for Curtis's masterwork, *Super Fly*, which would be his next album. On "Stone Junkie," he begins a conversation about the impact that drugs are starting to have on the Black community. In the late '60s, there was a simultaneous rise of both Black nationalist politics and the availability of underworld drugs like heroin and, to some extent, cocaine. Some in the Black community have suggested that the availability of these drugs was a bit too coincidental, and saw the timing of such things as part of a conspiracy to "medicate" the more radical and threatening influences of the Black power movement. "Stone Junkie" was a way into this conversation, and then the sound track for *Super Fly* would tackle the entire issue head-on. Considering the impact that drugs have had on inner-city America almost nonstop since the late '60s, one could say that Curtis was somewhat prophetic in the way that he used his music to explore the issue.

What is so striking about the *Super Fly* sound track—which

reached number one on both the pop charts and the R & B charts in 1972—is the fact that Curtis's music both functions with the film itself and also makes a mighty statement on its own. Over the years, I have encountered many people who know the sound track but have never seen the film. I have no problem in saying that the *Super Fly* sound track is one of the best albums and one of the best sound tracks of all time. Curtis's lyrics, compositions, and arrangements are just unbelievable and timeless. The album is like an extended urban suite that most effectively captures the mood of the time in an incredibly compelling fashion.

The opening sound in the film and on the sound track is "Little Child Running Wild," which immediately points to the fact that poverty is at the root of all social unrest and that drug use is like a necessary evil that emerges from this particular space otherwise known as the 'hood. Curtis describes a depressing "one-room shack/on the alley back." The "ghetto child" whom he refers to in the song is comparable to a barely-able-to-walk infant who has been dropped off in the middle of a jungle and forced to fend for himself. The song, both musically and lyrically, creates a vivid backdrop against which the movie is set and against which our imagination will be informed.

Curtis then moves on to the ghetto superhero known as the dope dealer or, in his parlance, "Pusherman." Priest, the main character in the film, is a cocaine dealer who is trying to get out of the game. This is the song that Curtis is singing when Priest walks into Scatter's nightclub in the film. For Curtis, the Pusherman is Everyman; he serves all roles and assumes all functions: "I'm your mama, I'm your daddy/I'm that nigga in the alley . . ." The Pusherman fills the gaps and voids in this jungle, providing escape from the harsh conditions, while making much bank in the process. Curtis describes the Pusherman's perspective as that of "just a hustler in spite of myself."

Here the dope dealer becomes an archetype for Black popular culture, and this leads to the continued presence of the drug dealer in hip hop culture. N.W.A.'s "Dope Man" is but one of many, many images of the dope dealer that refers back to Curtis's work on the sound track. The dope dealer is a charged figure, with both supporters and detractors, similar to the role that the Mafia figure has played in Italian American culture—and, by extension, American culture at large.

"Freddie's Dead" was the most successful single off the *Super Fly* sound track. It reached as high as number four on the pop charts and number two on the R & B charts. This song dealt with the impact of the dope game on one of its victims, the character Fat Freddy from the film. In the film, Fat Freddy is played by the actor Charles McGregor, who also appeared in a number of other films from that time period, including *Across 110th Street*.

Freddy is caught between a life of crime and his opportunistic wife, whom he attempts to control, to no avail. At one point, when Freddy is short with Priest's money, Priest threatens to "put that young girl of yours out there on whore's row tonight!" if Freddy doesn't come up with his paper. Freddy objects vehemently, and Priest sends him to do an armed robbery as a way of making up to him for coming up short with the cash. Later on in the film, Freddy gets arrested for beating a man with some brass knuckles because the man has hit on his wife. He snitches to the cops about Priest's operation and is later killed when he is hit by a car while trying to escape the police station. Freddy is quite pitiful, actually. He is weak and out of control, along with being intent on controlling his otherwise uncontrollable wife, who happens to be driving him crazy. His death is in many ways sympathetic, and indicative of those who are victimized by the game as opposed to those like Priest who are able to master it.

The song "Eddie You Should Know Better" is the only song on the sound track that is not in the film, but it is just as important as anything that does appear in the movie. Eddie is a reference to Priest's sidekick, the turncoat who snitches on Priest so that he can stay in the game himself. He is a classic playa hater. He puts his own self-interest over that of his partner. He is a disappointment to all involved.

"Eddie You Should Know Better" is followed on the album by "No Thing on Me." In the film, Priest goes to his old friend and mentor Scatter to buy some coke in what is his attempt to make one last big score before getting "out of the life." Scatter is initially hesitant, but he reluctantly agrees to help Priest out. As Priest leaves his meeting with Scatter we hear the song "No Thing on Me" playing in the club. The lyrics speak for themselves: "I'm so glad I've got my own/so glad that I can see... the man can't put no thing on me." This last score will allow Priest to leave the game on top, and Scatter's agreement to help him has basically granted him his independence. This decision is about self-determination, but it also has many implications for life beyond the film; many Black people in society were searching for the same kind of self-determination in society at large.

The sound track album ends with the title track, which is also the way the film itself ends. "Super Fly" was also a top ten pop single and top five R & B single. The song lays out Priest's philosophy and his mission in life, and this is basically distilled in the refrain "tryin' to get over," which is about survival, or as they say in hip hop, "just tryin' to eat." "Super Fly" is like the hustler's creed, and one could hear echoes of this when Biggie Smalls said the "hustler's prayer" in his song "Sky's the Limit." Priest's quest in the film for meaning in life is what informs the title song and makes it such a fitting conclusion to an incredible listening and viewing experience.

STEVIE WONDER

In 1971, Motown's child prodigy Stevie Wonder turned twenty-one and, as an adult, signed a new contract that allowed him to produce his own records. Often referred to as a "musical genius," he made a series of albums from 1972 to 1976 that could very easily be thought of as one long, extended musical meditation. With the release of *Music of My Mind* in 1972, to his magnum opus *Songs in the Key of Life* in 1976, and even beyond—going through to *Hotter Than July* in 1980—the man born Steveland Judkins, formerly known as Steveland Morris, who originally recorded under the moniker Little Stevie Wonder, created a musical body of work that will forever be hard to duplicate by any artist in any genre. In addition to all of his musical accomplishments, Wonder came to be known as a conscious figure whose socially inclined music and humanitarian efforts influenced many different causes, especially the recognition of Martin Luther King Jr.'s birthday as a national holiday, to which Wonder brought national attention with his song "Happy Birthday" in 1980.

In the early '70s, Stevie Wonder spent significant time recording in Electric Ladyland—the Manhattan studio in the Village that Jimi Hendrix had built with his own money—and in 1972 the material from that time in the famed studio appeared on the album *Music of My Mind*. In the Super Fly '70s, Stevie dominated the charts, producing a constant string of hit singles, including "Higher Ground" (1973), "Living for the City" (1973), "Superstition" (1973), "You Are the Sunshine of My Life" (1973), "Boogie on Reggae Woman" (1974), "You Haven't Done Nothing" (1974), "I Wish" (1977), "Sir Duke" (1977), and "Send One Your Love" (1979). Stevie won the Album of the Year Grammy Award for *Innervisions* in 1973, *Fullfillingness' First Finale* in 1974, and again for *Songs in the Key of Life* in 1976. Stevie has won twenty-two Grammy Awards during his career, as well as an Academy Award for his song "I Just Called to Say" in 1984 from the film *The Woman in Red*.

It was during this phase of his career in the '70s that Stevie established his reputation as one of the most creative artists ever, in both sound and style. Stevie's lyrics always veered between the conscious, the spiritual, and the political, while his own unique image set him apart and helped turn him into an icon for current and future generations.

One of the classics from this time period has to be Stevie's album *Talking Book* (1972). On the album cover, Stevie sits in a somewhat barren landscape, wearing cornrows, Indian jewelry, and a velvet afghan. His ethnically inspired dress is something that sets the image apart, pointing to the multicultural, spiritual quality that would inform his persona during this time.

The album itself is also a strong individual statement that demonstrates Stevie's ability to transcend the mundane and reach for something experimental. The result is ultimately much more satisfying in terms of its content. Like Marvin Gaye, Stevie felt stifled by Motown's assembly-line process, and he, too, after much intense negotiation with Barry Gordy, was able to produce his own music by singing, writing, and playing many of the instruments on the album. He was now finally able to achieve his own unique sound.

Stevie was one of the first artists to make extensive use of electronic sound effects in his music, making especially good use of both the clavinet keyboard and the Moog synthesizer, a device that turned electrical currents into musical sounds. This was similar to the way that Curtis Mayfield would use the wah-wah pedal like Jimi Hendrix to accentuate the sound of his guitar. Stevie tended to play several instruments on all his albums, and this was what made his sound so much his own. The liner notes of *Music of My Mind* say it best: "The man is his own instrument. The instrument is an orchestra." The playing of several instruments by a solo artist on the same album is also a method utilized regularly by Prince to great success throughout his musical career.

Stevie's work on *Innervisions* is especially poignant, and the signature work on this album of incredible tunes has to be "Living for the City." Similar in theme to both Curtis's "Little Child Running Wild" and Marvin's "Inner City Blues," this song touches on the migration of Southern Black people into the urban North and the difficult situations in which families found themselves as they live "just enough for the city." In other words, they were barely getting by. Survival was the best that they could hope for. This song is another example of the way that social consciousness defined a great deal of Black music in the early '70s.

On the album version of "Living for the City," there is an extended skit at the end that finds a young man getting off the bus in New York City, newly arrived from the South. Before he knows it, he is duped, caught up in a scam, then arrested by overly aggressive cops and sent to jail by a racist judicial system. When the skit ends Stevie comes back singing, but by this time his voice is hoarse, seemingly from singing his heart out about these really frustrating circumstances in this song, further adding to the emotion of the music and highlighting the extreme difficulties facing inner-city Black people of that day. This sobering plight underscored what was happening in America's cities as a result of White flight to the suburbs, a lowered tax base in the cities, and increasingly hostile treatment from the criminal justice system—especially for young Black men.

Stevie would cover similar territory in "Village Ghetto Land," a song on the *Songs in the Key of Life* album. This focus on the problems of urban America would be something that continued to inform Black music and certainly holds a great deal of significance in terms of hip hop culture. I have always thought that "Living for the City" served as an interesting template for Grand-Master Flash and the Furious Five's seminal hip hop track from 1982, "The Message." Public Enemy sampled "Living for the City," using the sounds of the prison guard slamming the cell door shut—"C'mon, get in the cell, nigger"—to open one of their greatest tracks, "Black Steel in the Hour of Chaos," from the landmark album *It Takes a Nation of Millions to Hold Us Back* (1988). Filmmaker Spike Lee turned Stevie's song into something like an extended music video, using it in *Jungle Fever* to underscore Wesley Snipes's Dante-esque journey into the heart of crack darkness while looking for his wayward brother, Gator, played brilliantly by Samuel L. Jackson.

ARETHA FRANKLIN

Does the Queen need an introduction? I think not. To call Aretha "the Queen of Soul" is to severely limit her importance. Aretha is the Queen of Music, period. There is no need to specify her reign according to a genre—she rules over all in the world of music and has for quite a long time.

Over a long career dating back to the early 1960s, Aretha has accumulated four platinum albums, eleven gold, and twenty-four number one hit singles on both the pop and R & B charts, while winning seventeen Grammy Awards in the process. Albums like *Aretha Live at Fillmore West* (1971), *Young, Gifted and Black* (1972), *Amazing Grace* (1972), and the sound track for the film *Sparkle* all earned gold status for her in the '70s, while singles like "Call Me" (1970), "Don't Play That Song" (1970), "Bridge over Troubled Water" (1971), "Spanish Harlem" (1971), "Angel" (1973), "I'm in Love" (1974), "Until You Come Back to Me" (1974), and "Something He Can Feel" (1976), were number one hits for her during the decade.

There is no better example of Aretha's versatility, though, than when she filled in for Luciano Pavarotti at the 1998 Grammy Awards. With less than ten minutes to rehearse, Aretha stepped onstage and belted out an aria so convincing that it seemed as though she had been singing opera all of her life.

Aretha was a big part of the Super Fly '70s. Her vibe, her energy, and her overall style were such that you cannot really deal with the era properly if you don't recognize and pay homage to her immense presence.

Aretha in many ways personified soul in every sense of that word. There is the religious notion of a "soul"—that which supersedes mind and body—and there is the cultural definition of *soul*, which has to do with one's essence, the core of one's being. Aretha qualifies for both. Her background in the Black church, growing up as the daughter of a powerful, politically connected minister, gave her the perfect opportunity to develop her musical talents in what was one of the primary incubators of Black talent at the time. Aretha was a native of Detroit, a city which itself had produced people like Joe Louis and Sugar Ray Robinson, religious institutions like the Nation of Islam, cultural institutions like Motown, and, in 1967, had been the site of one of the biggest urban riots in American history. Detroit at this time was a hotbed of Black creative energy. It most certainly provided an opportunity for its inhabitants to tap into this energy, and Aretha definitely did just that.

Aretha's father, the Reverend C. L. Franklin, was a prominent Black minister in the city and a close associate of Dr. Martin Luther King Jr. Reverend Franklin was one of the first Black ministers to enjoy a national reputation due to his popular radio programs that were heard throughout Black America. He was known as a skillful orator whose style drew many fans. One of his most famous sermons throughout the '50s and '60s was entitled "The Eagle Stirs the Nest."

Reverend Franklin's New Bethel Baptist Church was a place where many of the top gospel performers of the day came to show off their skills, so Aretha grew up in what amounted to a conservatory for gospel music. She witnessed firsthand the likes of Sam Cooke and the Ward Singers, and grew up not only watching these people perform, but she also had an extended connection to them and others because of her father's celebrity status in the Black community.

Aretha was signed by Columbia Records in the early '60s, and they envisioned her as a jazz singer. She could sing cookbook recipes and make them sound good, so the blues and jazz tunes she did were solid. Much of this material can be heard on a Columbia compilation entitled *Aretha Sings the Blues* that was released in 1980.

While Aretha sounds good on these records, it seems as though the record company had not really figured out what to do with her immense talents. Aretha was in need of a producer and some music that would allow her to fully explore the range of her vocal gifts. This would come some years later, when she signed with Ahmet Ertegun's Atlantic Records in 1967 and began work on a series of songs supervised by producer Jerry Wexler. Aretha went down to Muscle Shoals, Alabama, and began recording, only to leave at the behest of her controlling manager/husband, Ted White, after he and some of the White Southern band members got into a heated scuffle over some purported racial remarks. Aretha and Ted eventually went back to New York, but the musical process had already started.

These recording sessions would eventually lead to more, and soon Aretha released the first of a string of four records in 1967 that would immediately make her one of the top vocalists in America. Some of the classics of the Aretha Franklin catalog released at this time were "I Never Loved a Man," "Dr. Feelgood," "Chain of Fools," "A Natural Woman," and, of course, her most famous single, "Respect." These songs and many more would establish Aretha as the Queen of Soul in no uncertain terms.

In 1972, Aretha released the politically relevant *Young, Gifted and Black*, the title taken from a Langston Hughes poem. This was one of the first cassette tapes that I remember having as a kid, and it was part of the inspiration, along with *Lifestyles of the Rich and Famous*, for my own book *Young, Black, Rich and Famous*, which was published in 2003. *Young, Gifted and Black* featured a who's who of background singers and musicians who would come to be popular in their own right. These would include people like Donny Hathaway, Dr. John, Billy Preston, and Hubert Laws.

Aretha was continuing in the brilliant tradition of Ray Charles by taking gospel music and making it secular. She would eventually record a song, "Spirit in the Dark" (reprise with Ray

Charles), that appeared on her album *Aretha Live at Fillmore West*. This practice of transforming the gospel into secular music was at the heart of the musical genre that came to be known as soul, and was also connected to the multiple meanings of soul in both religious and cultural contexts. This process was very controversial in conservative Black churches. Many of these people criticized Aretha's decision to merge gospel and soul, as well as criticized her father for condoning it. Ray Charles had faced similar criticism, and so would many other Black artists who made the transition from the church to the outside world of popular music. Marvin Gaye's deep rift with his father, which resulted in his untimely death, was said to have started around the contentious issue of mixing the religious with the secular. This controversy was no small matter for many in the Black church.

Aretha released the gospel album *Amazing Grace* in 1972. This live concert album was recorded at the New Temple Missionary Baptist Church with the legendary gospel performer Reverend James Cleveland and the Southern California Community Choir. The album was all about Aretha getting back to her roots—and indeed she did. I have never been a fan of gospel music, but I would be suspect myself if I didn't recognize her incredible vocal skills along with those of the great Mahalia Jackson. Otherwise, I could do without the genre altogether. (I'm just keepin' it real here.) But, honestly, hearing Aretha sing on *Amazing Grace* might make Osama bin Laden momentarily consider converting to Christianity!

Aretha proved that after all of her success in the world of pop music, she could still go back home. She was in her element on the record. I've long thought that this return to her roots was something like an NBA superstar going back to play at the famed Rucker courts in Harlem. The record was released as a double album, and there's hardly a weak spot on it.

This record is arguably one of the greatest expressions of soul ever recorded! On it, Aretha moves through gospel standards like "Precious Memories," "Precious Lord," "Mary, Don't You Weep," "What a Friend We Have in Jesus," and, of course, the title track itself, "Amazing Grace." She also incorporates an incredible cover of Marvin Gaye's "Wholy Holy."

For me, one of the special moments on this record is hearing Reverend Franklin give oratorical weight to Aretha's performance. He speaks briefly, though effectively, and tells the adoring crowd that "Aretha is just a stone singer," and as far as he's concerned, she has "never left the church," directly addressing the concerns about her being too secular. The people in the audience that night strongly agreed with Reverend Franklin's assessment of his daughter's skills. His words echo the obvious, though: Aretha's voice has to be considered a national treasure, and her use of her instrument on the *Amazing Grace* album is some of the best musical work in the history of the American canon.

I would like to add that in the mid- to late '70s, Aretha had the pleasure of working with Curtis Mayfield on the sound track for the film *Sparkle*. Her collabo with Curtis brought together two giants of the era, and Aretha's work here is again of especially high quality, particularly on tracks like "Look into Your Heart" and "I Get High."

JAMES BROWN

To talk about the Super Fly '70s without talking about the God-father of Soul would be an omission of major proportions. Brown, who died on Christmas Day, 2006, had a career that spanned five decades, in which he accumulated ninety top–one hundred hits. Between 1959 and 1974, the Augusta, Georgia, native placed seventeen number one singles on the R & B chart. Though James Brown had his biggest impact in the '60s, his work in the early '70s—especially his work with his new backup band, the JB's—stands out for its amazingly funky music. His number one singles from the '70s include "Super Bad" (1970), "Hot Pants" (1971), "Make It Funky" (1971), "Get on the Good Foot" (1972), "Talking Loud and Saying Nothing" (1972), "My Thang" (1974), "Papa Don't Take No Mess" (1974), and "The Payback" (1974).

One of the things James Brown was known for over the years was the relentless manner in which he pushed his band. To say that James was a dictator is an incredible understatement. The wild stories of him fining his band members for missing notes while they were playing is just one example of the way that James sought perfection from his troops. In 1970, after a disagreement with the band over his tactics, James decided to prove a point. He sent for another group of musicians and flew them in on his private plane to play the gig, replacing the regulars. This new group of musicians was led by two brothers from Cincinnati, "Catfish" and his younger brother "Bootsy" Collins, along with bandleader and trombone player Fred Wesley. James introduced this band and its signature sound on the classic single "Sex Machine." Though members of the JB's seemed to come and go with a certain degree of frequency, the sound produced by this band, along with James doing his own thing vocally, was unmistakable. I am especially fond of the extended groove sessions the band included on the record, in which they would just extend the funk as if it were an improvisational jazz album. The song "Gonna Have a Funky Good Time" ("Doin' It to Death") is a great example of this type of playing. "Papa Don't Take No Mess" (1974) is another good example of the energized funky music that was being created in the early '70s. All in all, listening to James Brown and the JB's was an experience in and of itself.

One of my all-time favorites from this period happens to be James's attempt at an antidrug song, "King Heroin," in 1972. Over a slow groove, James, as only James can do, lays down his own philosophy about the impact that heroin is having on the inner city. Though heroin addiction was a serious matter at the time, listening to this song now is funny because James was so earnest in his plea, and because James was funny anyway, without trying to be. The man always had his own way with words. One need only remember Eddie Murphy's great imitations of James performing, on *Saturday Night Live*, to conjure up the humor.

Another good example of James's unique mouthpiece is quite apparent in the 1996 Muhammad Ali documentary *When We Were Kings*. The film features James circa 1975, when he was in Zaire performing as part of the festivities surrounding the Ali/Foreman "Rumble in the Jungle" fight. James, who is in conversation with Don King, begins to talk about the unfairness of racism by pointing out the hypocrisy inherent in America's racial politics, which is characterized by mentioning someone being able to "take advantage of your woman, Jack, and you can't even speak to his." He closes out his rant by boldly declaring, "Do unto others as you would have somebody do unto you. And I don't have to use the word FM backwards!"

Another one of my favorites joints from the James Brown catalog of the Super Fly '70s is the ultraclassic *The Payback* (1974). James released the movie sound tracks to both *Black Caesar* and *Slaughter's Big Rip-Off* (1973), and he was set to do another one for Larry Cohen, the director of *Black Caesar*, but Cohen for reasons not disclosed rejected his contribution. Can you imagine someone rejecting a James Brown record? The unmitigated gall! James later released this music as the album *The Payback*.

James exhorted his listeners to get ready for the "big payback," and seemed to say it all when he said, "Don't do me no damn favor/I don't know karate/but I know krazor." The word *krazor* is, of course, a combination of *crazy* and *razor*, and so James was saying that unlike so many others of that time who were immersed in martial arts, he knew something else, a bit more old-school, but perhaps much more lethal.

James's influence on the hip hop generation is widespread, and both he and George Clinton provided much of the source material for hip hop producers to sample throughout the '80s and '90s. There are so many of these samples that one could do a book just listing these songs, but I want to point out two examples that stand out for me. The first is from the Detroit hip hop group Slum Village on their track "I Don't Know" (2000), on which producer Jazzy Jeff—who is better known for his association with Will Smith but who is a great producer in his own right—samples James's voice in a clever call and response that serves as the song's hook. The other song I would like to call attention to is Nas's opening track on his *God's Son* (2002) album, "Get Down." It uses a sample from "The Boss," a song that James originally recorded for the sound track of *Black Caesar*, the 1973 Fred Williamson blaxploitation film. "The Boss" is also used quite well in *American Pimp* as an introduction to Bishop Don "Magic" Juan, the former pimp–turned-preacher who has become a familiar figure in contemporary hip hop circles.

One of the key elements to the Super Fly '70s was soul, and James had this in abundance—not only in the music itself, but in the overall style that he affected onstage and throughout his life in general. His hair, from the perm of the '60s to the 'fro of the '70s; his fashion sense, like the double-knit green jump suit, open at the chest, with the acronym GFOS (Godfather of Soul) on the waistband that he wears in *When We Were Kings*; and his signature and often imitated dance moves and his out-of-this-world showmanship all help to explain why James was known as Soul Brother Number One. There would be no Michael Jackson, no Prince, and there would have never been an MC Hammer, were it not for the model James Brown established. This is what makes him an icon of the Super Fly '70s.

QUINCY JONES

I remember when I first began hearing the name Quincy Jones back in the Super Fly '70s. I was always curious about what he really did, because even though his name was quite popular, he wasn't a singer and he wasn't known for playing his trumpet anymore. I was uncertain. My young-ass mind had no conception of what a producer was. It turns out that I was not the only one uncertain about what the man who came to be known as Q did back in the day. The reason no one outside of the record business knew what a producer was had to do with the fact that Black people up until then had been almost exclusively confined to performing. Q, though, took it to another level.

"The Dude"—which is the title of one of his more famous albums from 1980—charted a path that demonstrated one could have a major impact on the industry and the culture, working creatively to shape projects and guide careers, above and beyond the always transitory nature of attempting to succeed as a performer. Q's success in the business suite and in the studio would make him one of the most significant creative figures in the history of American popular culture, as evidenced by his 2001 selection as a Kennedy Center honoree. His pioneering efforts as a composer for film and television sound tracks were so far ahead of their time in the '60s and '70s that it's hard even to fathom now. If ever the term *Renaissance man* applied to someone, that someone would most certainly be Quincy Jones.

Quincy Jones had his most considerable impact on creatively shaping the '70s from behind the scenes. What has always been so remarkable about Q is the fact that he has been able to spread his influence and make his mark on so many different areas of the culture, in the Super Fly '70s and beyond, specifically in music, film, and television. During the course of his career, Q has been the triple threat of entertainment. He has worked with a veritable who's who of performers from across several genres of music. These include Cannonball Adderley, Louis Armstrong, George Benson, Diahann Carroll, his close friend Ray Charles, Sammy Davis, Aretha Franklin, Dizzy Gillespie, Frank Sinatra, Sarah Vaughan, Ice-T, Melle Mel, Barry White, Donna Summer, Lesley Gore, Little Richard, and Peggy Lee, among many, many others.

I mean, think about it: Who else but Q could have gotten practically every significant musical artist of the era together to record "We Are the World" (1984) to support famine relief in Ethiopia? Q "discovered" Oprah and produced *The Color Purple* (1985), and later cast a young Will Smith in *The Fresh Prince of Bel-Air* (1990–96), putting both of them on track to become the superstars they are today. And just to show that he was not all about pop, he had enough foresight and street cred to start *Vibe* magazine in the '90s. So far he has won twenty-nine Grammys, and three of those were for Producer of the Year in 1981, 1983, and 1990.

In the '50s and the '60s, Q made the transition from jazz trumpet player, bandleader, composer, songwriter, and producer to record executive, becoming vice president of Mercury Records in 1964 and the first African American to hold such a prominent place on a major label in the mainstream music industry. He eventually made his way to Hollywood to do something else unheard-of for a Black man at the time—film scoring. He composed the scores for major Hollywood hits like *The Pawnbroker* (1964), *In Cold Blood* (1967), and *Bob & Carol & Ted & Alice* (1969), in addition to scoring the Sidney Poitier films *In the Heat of the Night* (1967) and *For the Love of Ivy* (1968). So when the Super Fly '70s began, Q was on an incredible and unprecedented roll as he began to expand his range across all the areas of culture.

During the '70s, Q released several albums under his own name. These include *Cactus Flower* (1969), *Gula Matari* (1970), *They Call Me Mister Tibbs* (1970), *Smackwater Jack* (1971), *You've Got It Bad, Girl* (1973), *The Hot Rock* (1972), *Body Heat* (1974), *Mellow Madness* (1975), *I Heard That!* (1976), *Sounds . . . and Stuff Like That* (1978), and *The Wiz* (1978). He also guided and nurtured the careers of George and Louis Johnson, who recorded as the Brothers Johnson, working with them on albums like *Look Out for #1* (1976), *Right on Time* (1977), which featured the popular love song "Strawberry Letter 23"—a song in which the actual title is never uttered—and *Blam* (1978). He also produced Rufus, featuring Chaka Kahn on the album *MasterJam* (1979).

Q's biggest record as a producer in the '70s was the blockbuster *Off the Wall* (1979), the album that began his especially successful collaborative efforts working with the self-proclaimed "King of Pop," Michael Jackson. Q would come to dominate the game as he went on to produce both *Thriller* (1982), the biggest record in history, as well as *Bad* (1987) with Michael in the 1980s. The overwhelming success of *Off the Wall*, which is said to have sold in the range of twenty million albums worldwide since its original release, would establish Q as the most powerful producer in the music business for years to come.

Q had initially worked with Michael Jackson on the film *The Wiz*, which was originally a Broadway play. It had now become a Motown Productions film written by Joel Schumacher and directed by Sidney Lumet, the latter of whom Q had also worked with on *The Pawnbroker*. *The Wiz* used an all–African American cast in its adaptation of *The Wizard of Oz*. In addition to Jackson's role as Scarecrow, the film also starred Diana Ross, Lena Horne, Nipsey Russell, and Richard Pryor. Q served as music supervisor and music producer on the film, which also allowed him to work with notable writers/performers Nick Ashford and Valerie Simpson, along with a then-unknown Luther Vandross.

Q also established himself in the world of television during this time. He composed the theme and scored the Raymond Burr crime drama *Ironside* (1967–75), which came to be a familiar theme, and this would eventually be used again in Tarantino's film *Kill Bill*. Q also cowrote the theme song "Hikky Burr" with Bill Cosby and scored the series *The Bill Cosby Show*, which debuted on NBC in 1969. Perhaps Q's best known and most memorable theme song ever was the one he created for *Sanford and Son*, which debuted in 1972. And later, thanks to his work in the groundbreaking miniseries *Roots* (1977), he would win an Emmy Award for Outstanding Achievement in Music Composition for a Series.

It's important to point out that Q even survived a cerebral aneurysm in 1974. He had to undergo two different brain surgeries and was forced to stop playing the trumpet because of this.

But his time away from the scene was only temporary, as he seemed to come back even stronger.

Ultimately Quincy Jones, like Gordon Parks, demonstrated that there was something for African Americans beyond performing, and in so doing he inspired future generations to follow his lead. The ability to influence what we hear and see is an indication of one's position in the game, and Q certainly stands tall in this regard.

JIMI HENDRIX, *BAND OF GYPSIES* (1970)

Though many people would never consider Jimi Hendrix to be a part of the Super Fly '70s, his place in the game must be acknowledged. It was always ironic to me that one of the world's best-known Black musical artists has rarely been regarded as a part of the canon of Black music. Hendrix, of course, has almost exclusively been associated with rock music, and while his status as such is without question, I would like to reclaim his legacy here. Hendrix is without a doubt a major part of the Super Fly '70s, and his live album *Band of Gypsies* is one of the main reasons why.

Jimi Hendrix cut his musical teeth playing guitar in blues and R & B bands, both in his native Seattle and also while stationed in Kentucky during his stint in the army. Professionally, some of his early gigs were with well-known Black artists like Little Richard and the Isley Brothers. At his core, Hendrix was a master blues musician whose avant-garde approach to his instrument allowed him to transcend any routine categories, but this, in many ways, is also what led to his being embraced by rock, at what seemed to be the expense of being highly regarded in Black music circles.

Timing was also part of the reason why Hendrix was never really thought of in terms of Black music. He happened to come along at the height of the surging demands emboldened by the Black power movement. The militancy and the racially exclusive ideology of the moment meant that anyone or anything not considered to be unquestionably Black would not get any attention. Furthermore, Hendrix was not only seen as playing "White" music, but he was also seen playing in all-White settings, with an all-White band known as the Jimi Hendrix Experience. In other words, there was little need for a Jimi Hendrix in a world dominated by the ultra-Black image of someone like James Brown.

While the racial politics of the era are to be taken into account, the passage of time means that we can now consider Hendrix anew, in light of both historical distance and changing societal perceptions.

In 1969, Hendrix put together another group known as the Band of Gypsies. The group included two Black musicians, Buddy Miles on drums and Hendrix's homie from his army days, bassist Billy Cox. The racial composition of the band was in stark contrast to the all-White makeup of the Experience. Hendrix wanted a different sound, and this new group would provide the opportunity for this.

The Band of Gypsies were set to perform four concerts over two nights at Fillmore East in New York starting on New Year's Eve, 1969. The songs that made up the album *Band of Gypsies* are taken from the shows on January 1, 1970. The album opens with an incredibly funky blues joint called "Who Knows"; the track culminates with some crazy-ass high-pitched Buddy Miles lyrics and an accompanying chant. This sets the tone for an incredible aural experience in which Jimi more than demonstrates his immersion in the blues idiom and his indelible link to the very best of the Black musical tradition. Another standout track on the record is the amazing "Machine Gun," a tune in which Hendrix shows off his ability to make his instrument speak well beyond its intended usage. He is able to make the guitar sound exactly like a machine gun, echoing the sound of gunfire that had become so familiar, thanks to the ubiquity of the Vietnam War, to the American consciousness of the times.

This phenomenal group with its amazing sound was documented on only this one album. Appearing at Madison Square Garden in late January of 1970, Hendrix came onstage visibly high, disconnected, and unable to mount an effective performance. The Band of Gypsies was broken up not long after this, and he re-formed the old Experience. Some have suggested that Hendrix was given a highly potent form of acid on purpose so as to hasten the breakup of the group. It was thought that there was a desire to have Hendrix return to his old band and start making music again that would appeal to his previous audience. The obvious racial implications of such a theory do seem plausible. I remember hearing Buddy Miles say as much in a documentary on Hendrix; it played on a continuous loop at the Experience Music Project, which is a hip music museum in Hendrix's hometown of Seattle that was created by former Microsoft cofounder, billionaire Paul Allen.

It is also important to point out that Hendrix was a clean

muthafucka in his own right. His own unique style of dress was a cross between hippie chic and pimp fashion, all accented by his famous bandannas. All of this, coupled with his easily identifiable Afro and the mellow, laid-back sound of his voice, makes him one of the coolest cats ever, and an icon whose legacy must be held in high esteem among all those who celebrate the Super Fly '70s.

RICK JAMES

"I'm Rick James, bitch!" This has to be the best line of 2004. When comedian Dave Chappelle uttered these famous words on his television show, he not only served up one of the funniest skits in American comedy history, he also brought light back onto one of the most Super Fly figures from the '70s, funkmaster extraordinaire and world-class hedonist Rick James. Unfortunately, Rick died later that year, but not before being reborn once again in a career that never had a dull moment.

But the man originally known as James Ambrose Johnson Jr. is more than just a punch line from a funny skit; he is one of the most significant Black musical artists of the era right before hip hop started its takeover of American culture. Rick, a native of Buffalo and the nephew of Melvin Franklin of the Temptations, in some ways helped to make the transition from funk to hip hop—if not entirely in his music, then most certainly with his don't-give-a-fuck attitude. Rick James was one of the first Black male performers to sport cornrows, a style that has its roots in Africa, the penitentiary, and on the front porches of many Black households throughout America. Though the style would become common in the hip hop era, especially among rappers and NBA players, Rick was sportin' braids back in the late '70s, before they regained popularity in the mid-'90s.

Rick was born in Buffalo, New York, and originally started performing there as a teenager before joining the naval reserve, only to go AWOL and eventually flee to Canada to continue practicing his craft as a musical artist. While in Canada in 1964, he started a band called the Mynah Birds, a band that at one point even included the famous rock-and-roller Neil Young. Rick later joined Motown Records in the late '60s as a songwriter and a producer, before he pursued his own musical direction as a performer.

In 1978, he released his solo debut, *Come Get It,* which featured classics like "You and I" and the weed-smoking anthem "Mary Jane." Rick celebrated his love for gettin' blazed and spawned a cottage industry, a truly large following of imitators over the years. These include Dr. Dre, who named a whole album *The Chronic*; D'Angelo, who dropped the brilliant single "Brown Sugar"; and the rapper Styles P, who laid it down his way with the track "Good Times." The Queen of Hip Hop Soul, Mary J. Blige, shortened the title and sampled the original, creating the sound of her own name, Mary J. This became a signature part of her performances as well.

After the success of *Come Get It,* Rick released *Bustin' out of L7* (1979), which was his attempt to break away from convention, as indicated by the "L7" designation. If you put L and 7 together you get a square, and Rick wanted to go outside of the box and move away from all "squares" as well. A square, of course, was a term popularized during the heyday of jazz music in this country, and it referred to those who were outside or opposite of what was considered hip. A square was a conventional muthafucka—in other words, someone who represented the epitome of mainstream boredom and an overall lack of consciousness about anything considered cool and hip. This was what Rick wanted to break away from. It's ironic, but Rick's label, Motown, was, in the early '70s, square in terms of what they wanted, until Marvin Gaye and Stevie Wonder managed to break through to Barry Gordy and change the course of music history. Rick James was the beneficiary of this more liberal approach.

The crazy world of Rick James moved far beyond the '70s, though. It was in 1981 that he released his best work ever, the concept album *Street Songs*. The song "Super Freak" would come to define Rick's career for a lot of people, and the rock-inspired joint also received an added boost from the success that rapper MC Hammer got when he used the song as a sample for his megahit "Can't Touch This" in the early '90s.

"Super Freak," though, was nothing compared to most of Rick's other tracks on *Street Songs*. His duet with Teena Marie, one of the most soulful White chicks to ever live, will stand forever, while a track like "Ghetto Life" set the table for gangsta rap and its emphasis on the highs and lows of life in the 'hood that was to emerge in the late '80s. "Standing on the Top" featured a tight-ass Temptations collabo, too. All in all, *Street Songs* is a thorough masterpiece that reminds one of the early '70s. Concept albums like this were more common then than in the disco-hangover days of the early '80s, when such things seemed to have passed away.

Though he continued to produce hits after *Street Songs*,

Rick's career seemed to slow down quite a bit. He did find himself producing acts like Teena Marie and The Mary Jane Girls, as well as Eddie Murphy's feeble attempt at music stardom in the mid-'80s, *Party All the Time*.

In the early '90s, however, Rick was back in the news when he was charged with assaulting two different women, one of whom accused him of burning her with a hot crack pipe during one of his prolonged binges. After serving some time, Rick returned and generally stayed below the radar until the Chappelle skit skyrocketed him back into relevance. His loud, funky, flamboyant, and irreverent spirit will forever be remembered, as will his unforgettable music. For many people Rick is best known for his cocaine-fueled antics, and it appears that his colorful, over-the-top life will likely overshadow his talents as an artist. For this reason he remains one of the most underrated musical artists of his era, and he will probably never get his due in this regard, because people tend to remember the tabloidlike salaciousness of his persona at the expense of recognizing his creative substance.

BARRY WHITE

The man with perhaps the most recognizable voice in America was none other than "the Maestro" himself, Barry White. The former Los Angeles gang member came to be known as a bedroom balladeer of the highest order. Barry's large frame and especially deep voice came to be synonymous with smooth seduction and an all-encompassing sexually oriented vibe. The endless stories about children conceived with Barry's music as the sound track continue unto this day.

On a more personal note, Barry's name has long come up when women wanted to make reference to my own voice. I resisted this for a long time, because even though I got mad love for Barry, I like to think of myself as the unique nigga that I am. But after hearing this so many times, I eventually gave in and realized that there is nothing bad about being linked with Big Barry— nothing at all. Though I too possess the "platinum baritone," I have to give props where they're due. So here's a big shout-out to the memory of the late Barry White for paving the way for a big man with a deep voice to get love in America! Respect!

In the '60s, Barry worked with an all-girl group modeled after the Supremes called Love Unlimited. He eventually produced, arranged, and wrote "Walking in the Rain (With the One I Love)," which became a hit song for the group. Then, in the '70s, Barry was working on some demos for a male lead for Love Unlimited when his record company thought it would be a good idea for him to sing the songs himself. Barry (who had also been a backup singer) moved out front, turned Love Unlimited into an orchestra, and started on the journey that would make his voice a household sound.

After expanding Love Unlimited into the Love Unlimited Orchestra, complete with live musicians and a heavy string section, Barry scored a major hit with his arrangement and production on the instrumental "Love's Theme" in 1974. He also had much success with tracks like "I'm Gonna Love You Just a Little Bit More" (1973), "Never, Never Gonna Give You Up" (1973), "Can't Get Enough of Your Love, Babe" (1974), and "It's Ecstasy

When You Lay Down Next to Me" (1977), among many others throughout the '70s.

Barry scored a major comeback in the '90s with his album *The Icon Is Love* (1994), and his music and his voice came to be integral parts of the hit television show *Ally McBeal* (1997–2002) at that time as well. The character of the deep-voiced Chef on the animated show *South Park* (1997–present) was also created with Big Barry in mind, though he declined to serve as the voice of the character. However, this opened the way for another deep-voiced brotha, Isaac Hayes, to provide the voice and vibe of *South Park's* Chef.

The thing about Barry is that his voice and the way he carried himself came to be signatures of his overall significance in the culture at large. Women swooned at the sound of his deep baritone and the feelings of sensuality that it induced. Barry cultivated the image of the big man as a smooth playa who could seduce chicks simply by the sound of his voice, and this image would, in many ways, inform the aura surrounding a larger-than-life rapper like Biggie Smalls many years later, as evidenced by his classic remix of "One More Chance" (1995).

Barry White died in 2003 from kidney failure.

HERBIE HANCOCK

Even though most of the musical artists who stood out in the '70s did so for their ability to articulate their own unique vision through performing, writing, and producing, Herbie Hancock stands out because he made the transition from straight-ahead jazz to fusion and then to funk, helping to push these transitions with his innovations. His albums the platinum-selling *Head Hunters* (1973) and *Thrust* (1974) are both exemplary of his unquestioned status during this decade.

Herbie, while still in his early twenties, began to get a great deal of attention at the start of the '60s for his work on the famous Blue Note jazz label. Among the well-known and influential records that he made during this time was *Empyrean Isles* (1964), featuring the song "Cantaloupe Island," which became the basis for a new hit single in the early '90s when the group US3 reworked the song on a hip hop tip. The incredible *Maiden Voyage* (1965) followed on the heels of *Empyrean*, with the title track itself becoming a jazz standard. *Maiden Voyage* has to be one of the mellowest records ever recorded, and the Freddie Hubbard trumpet solo on the title track is nothing short of unbelievable.

During this time, Herbie caught the eye of the great Miles Davis, and Miles selected him to be the pianist for his new quintet. This quintet, which also featured Ron Carter on bass, a seventeen-year-old Tony Williams on drums, and Wayne Shorter on the saxophone, came to be known as Miles's second great quintet, after an earlier group that included John Coltrane, Red

albums that merged the sounds of fusion with more of a funk base. Possibly because Herbie was younger and more in tune with this energy, his albums were able to reach a younger Black urban audience, an audience that Miles was never quite able to reach with similar forays on an album like *On the Corner* (1972).

Both *Head Hunters* and *Thrust* feature long, extended tracks that flow nicely from one to the next. These always remind me of the era when serious music listeners owned reel-to-reel tape players that would allow you to listen to an almost endless stream of music without breaking the mood. In many ways, Herbie's music on these two albums is the perfect accompaniment to the Super Fly '70s era. Tracks like "Chameleon," "Butterfly," and Herbie's reworking of his jazz classic "Watermelon Man" stand out on these albums, but the entire experience is one that should be had for all those interested in dealing with some fly-ass music.

Herbie's innovations would continue into the '80s, when he became one of the first musicians to experiment with the Apple computer in his music. In 1983, Herbie dropped another classic, which once again exposed a new musical twist to the unsuspecting masses. With the release of his Grammy-winning single "Rockit" (1983), Herbie, along with Grandmaster DXT, demonstrated the hip hop practice of scratchin' on a popular record and ignited an interest in the art of turntableism, which is the use of a turntable as an improvisational musical instrument. The video for the song was also an early favorite on the fledgling MTV network, even though Hancock's absence from the video was due to the network's reluctance in their early days to highlight Black performers. However, after Michael Jackson's videos from the *Thriller* album helped to make the network, their policies slowly began to change to the point that now MTV is as much a hip hop channel as anything else.

AL GREEN

Another of the great voices of the Super Fly '70s is a man who moved freely between soul and gospel music, often combining the two genres in his own distinct way. This man is none other than Al Green. Al Green in the '70s would join a long line of singers, past and present, like the Staple Singers, Aretha Franklin, Sam Cooke, Ray Charles, Marvin Gaye, and Donny Hathaway, who often blurred the lines between the sacred and the secular in their musical approach.

Green, a Forrest City, Arkansas, native, teamed up with producer and label head Willie Mitchell in 1969 and signed with Mitchell's Hi Records, based in Memphis, Tennessee. Green drew attention with his single "I'm Tired of Being Alone" in 1971. Then he dropped two great albums back to back: the gold album *Let's Stay Together* and the platinum-selling album *I'm Still in Love with You,* both of which were released in 1972, and both of which produced number one R & B singles with their respective title tracks. On the cover of *I'm Still in Love with You* Al Green is resplendent, dressed all in white from head to toe, sitting in a white wicker chair. He continued to make some serious soul ballads through 1975, scoring more hits with singles like "You Ought to Be with Me" (1972), "Look What You've Done for Me" (1972), "Call Me" (1973), "Here I Am" (1973), "Sha-

La-La" (1974), "Let's Get Married" (1974), "Livin' for You" (1974), "Full of Fire" (1975), and "L-O-V-E" (1975). Standing as one of the truly great singers and distinct voices of his era, Al Green worked his gospel feel into some sensual tunes that were all about carnal pursuits.

In 1974, at the height of his fame, Green suffered a setback that was as bizarre as it was tragic. While he was taking a shower, his girlfriend at the time, Mary Woodson, came into the bathroom and poured a pot of scalding-hot grits over his body, causing Green to sustain second-degree burns. She then walked into another room of the house and committed suicide. Green was so shaken up by this that he eventually stopped singing soul music and moved into gospel, even opening up his own church, the Full Gospel Tabernacle, in Memphis, where he has been entrenched ever since. Though he has, on occasion, returned to recording secular music, he has remained a minister and a gospel artist.

There is a classic piece of footage of Al Green from the '70s performing on *Soul Train* and wearing a tricked-out suit in Albert and Allen Hughes's film *Dead Presidents*.

THE ISLEY BROTHERS

You know you're the shit when you have a group that spans six decades. The brothers Isley have been recording in one incarnation or another since the late 1950s and have scored hits in every decade from the '50s through the present, which is nothing short of amazing.

The original core group formed in 1954 and consisted of Ronald, O'Kelly, Rudolph, and Vernon. Vernon died in a motorcycle accident in 1957, and after a short breakup, the three remaining brothers formed a trio. In 1973 they added younger brothers Ernie and Marvin, along with their brother-in-law Chris Jasper. In 1984, the younger members broke away to form another group known as Isley Jasper Isley. O'Kelly died of a heart attack in 1986, Rudolph left performing to become a minister shortly thereafter, while Ronald pursued a solo career until reunited with Ernie and Marvin, re-creating the Isley Brothers in 1991. Marvin left the group in 1997 due to complications that arose from diabetes, yet Ronald and Ernie have carried on into the present.

This seemingly endless supply of Isley Brothers has consistently altered the makeup of the group, but it has never seemed to matter. The group and the name Isley have become closely connected to the evolution of Black music, from the early days of rock and roll to hip hop in the present. Considering all the trouble the Jacksons have had over the years, it might be a safer bet to pick the Isleys as the royal family of Black popular music.

The Isley Brothers released a string of albums in the '70s that both charted new territory for them and helped to define and create the overall Super Fly aura that spanned the decade. In 1973, the band who recorded on their own T-Neck record label signed a distribution deal with Columbia, and it was also around this same time that the older brothers made their younger siblings full-fledged members of the band, with the younger brothers and brother-in-law Chris Jasper providing the musical accompaniment. From '73 forward they released *3 + 3* (1973), *Live It Up*

(1974), *The Heat Is On* (1975), *Harvest for the World* (1976), *Go for Your Guns* (1977), *Showdown* (1978), and the two-album set *Winner Takes All* (1979), all of which are platinum-selling albums, except for the gold album *Live It Up*. The Isleys had a long list of hit singles during this time also, which include "That Lady" (1973), "Summer Breeze" (1974), "Fight the Power" (1975), "For the Love of You" (1975), "Harvest for the World" (1976), "Living in the Life" (1977), "The Pride" (1977), and "Take Me to the Next Phase" (1978). I have always thought that the Isley Brothers were a great album band and were best appreciated in this way. Their unique blend of love ballads, hard-charging funk, and socially conscious statements like their famous number one hit "Fight the Power" gave them a distinct edge as one of the top groups of their time.

"Fight the Power," released in 1975, confronted America's inept leadership during the post-Watergate era. The Isley Brothers' cynical response to getting the "big runaround" from the powers-that-be led them to label all government efforts as "bullshit going down." When the single for the song was sent to urban radio unedited, many stations played the song as delivered, which caused a major controversy, as records with explicit language were fairly uncommon at the time and certainly weren't aired on the radio.

It makes sense, then, that "Fight the Power" and its disregard for language standards of the day would have such an impact on hip hop culture many years later. In 1989, Public Enemy used the song's title as their inspiration in creating the theme song for Spike Lee's brilliantly confrontational *Do the Right Thing*. The idea of fighting the power proved to be a political sentiment that has long informed Black protest in one form or another, and the Isley Brothers' hit song became a powerful anthem of the Super Fly '70s.

The Isley Brothers were also known for their pimped-out fashion and for often sportin' vivid colors, velvet, Super Fly collars, neatly trimmed Afros, and platform shoes on their album covers. They often looked like barons of the 'hood in their regal attire, and it appeared that one of their former bandmates, Jimi Hendrix, and his own unique fashion sense had a strong and lasting influence on their style as well.

The music of the Isley Brothers has long been popular in the world of rap music, with Ice Cube's use of their hit single "Footsteps in the Dark" as the sample for his incredible "It Was a Good Day," and Biggie Smalls's use of "Between the Sheets" in the hit "Big Poppa" being some of the true classics in the history of hip hop. Further, Ronald Isley redefined himself in the mid-'90s and created an alter ego in the image of an old-school gangsta kingpin known as Mr. Bigg. This all came about as a result of his collaborations with producer R. Kelly. Mr. Bigg and the Isley Brothers continually made themselves relevant to a new generation of followers through their songs and videos, even scoring a number one album on the pop charts in 2003 with the release of *Body Kiss*.

THE OHIO PLAYERS

One of the hottest funk bands of the Super Fly '70s was none other than the Ohio Players. These cats from Dayton, Ohio, were originally known as the Ohio Untouchables. Throughout the '60s they worked as a backup band for a variety of soul singers, including Wilson Pickett. The group reached their stride in the mid-'70s, when they signed with Mercury Records in 1974 and then went on to release a string of funky hits between 1974 and 1977, which include "Skin Tight," "Fire," "I Wanna Be Free," "Heaven Must Be Like This," "Love Rollercoaster," "Sweet Sticky Thing," and "Who'd She Coo?," among others. Both "Fire" and "Love Rollercoaster" reached number one on the R & B and the pop charts. The Ohio Players helped to put the Buckeye State on the musical map, as did other artists of this time, like the Isley Brothers, Bootsy Collins, the O'Jays, and Slave.

The lead singer and most recognizable voice belonged to Leroy "Sugarfoot" Bonner, who also played guitar. Sugarfoot sang in a down-home drawl, and he was known for his exaggerated beggin' and pleadin', which were set against the band's high-pitched falsetto hooks and their own unique brand of Midwestern gutbucket funk. Sugarfoot's most recognizable trait was his signature "Oww gurl" line, which punctuated many of the band's hits and was widely copied by others like Lionel Richie when he was with the Commodores, as well as Larry Blackmon of Cameo. Though Sugarfoot was the lead singer, he wasn't necessarily the face of this unit, which really functioned like a collective, as the entire band was accorded both writing and producing credits on their albums.

The Ohio Players were always fly beyond imagination, and their hits scored on both urban radio and on the pop charts as well. In addition to their funky sounds, though, the Ohio Players were also well-known for their sexually provocative album covers. The group's label, Mercury Records, hired *Playboy* magazine photographer Richard Fegley to do the layout for the album covers of *Skin Tight, Honey, Mr. Mean,* and *Gold.* On each cover there appeared a seductively nude Black woman, who, though covered up in all the right places, still struck a series of sexually provocative poses that made these album covers famous. This became a signature look for the band and helped to enshrine them as the playas implied in their title. The album covers were actually more popular than photos of the group.

The album cover for *Honey* occupied its own place in urban legend. Cover model and former *Playboy* centerfold Esther Cordet appeared completely nude, taking a dip of honey on the outside cover, and was seen completely covered in honey on the inside of the jacket. Rumors began to spread that Cordet was burned by the honey and also developed a bad skin rash because of it. The rumors eventually got worse when it was said that she was murdered during the recording of *Love Rollercoaster* as a result of her demands for compensation from the record label. According to these stories, you could actually hear her screaming right before the second verse of the song.

Though this was all highly unsubstantiated urban myth, it was never confirmed one way or the other by the group or the record label, allowing the mystery to develop a life of its own. This helped to solidify the group as purveyors of the sexually outrageous and, as one would expect, also helped record sales.

GIL SCOTT-HERON (GSH)

While the Super Fly '70s has been very kind to hip hop culture in general, the artist known as Gil Scott-Heron is undoubtedly hip hop's godfather. Some people have tried to force Gil Scott-Heron into a place in hip hop that is just not accurate; for example, calling him the first rapper.

GSH is not a rapper, though. His work certainly set the table for what would become hip hop, but he was not part of the culture itself. However, he was an integral part of what immediately preceded hip hop, and it was this that hip hop has so liberally borrowed from. Gil Scott-Heron's work as a poet, spoken-word artist, and as an overall lyricist is without question some of the most influential, insightful, and inspiring music ever recorded. This, along with the Last Poets and the Watts Prophets, functioned collectively to inspire hip hop as it began to emerge in the mid-'70s.

In 1970, Heron released his first album, entitled *Small Talk at 125th and Lenox,* which featured him reading from his book of poetry, backed by a group of musicians. One of the pieces was a polemic against the increasing prevalence of the mass media called "The Revolution Will Not Be Televised." Though this title has been appropriated in multiple ways since then, very few people actually know what the real song says. "The Revolution Will Not Be Televised" has to be one of the most astute critiques of the media ever articulated, as he goes on about the numbness that the media has engendered in the minds of the masses, especially mainstream White America. In many ways, the song prefigures the great Public Enemy critique "Don't Believe the Hype," from their 1998 classic *It Takes a Nation of Millions to Hold Us Back.*

While "The Revolution" seems perhaps a bit dated today due to its specific references, its spirit is alive and well. An overdose of the media can be a dangerous thing, but, in spite of GSH's predictions, it seems that the media has even coopted the notion of revolution. Nothing can stop the media's forward motion. But Gil Scott's point is still well taken.

On the same album, Heron did another piece called "Whitey on the Moon," in which he exposed the irony and the contradictions inherent in the idea of the amount of resources put into the space program during the Cold War, while millions of the nation's citizens suffered unquestionable despair right here on earth.

He released his second album, *Pieces of a Man,* in 1971, and he would go on to release a series of records through the '70s and into the '80s. He scored hits with *Johannesburg* (1975), bringing attention to the plight of Black South Africans long before it became a well-known issue in the '80s; *In the Bottle;* and *Angel Dust,* his spiel on the dangers of the drug PCP. Gil Scott-Heron managed to shine a light on many issues facing inner-city Black communities. This brand of social consciousness most certainly influenced a future generation of conscientious hip hop artists like Chuck D, Ice Cube, Mos Def, and Common, among many others. Kanye West samples Gil Scott-Heron's "Home Is Where the Hatred Is" on his 2005 record *Late Registration,* reminding listeners that the well never runs dry when dealing with an artist of GSH's magnitude.

One of my favorite joints, though, actually came out in the early '80s, right as rap music was starting to move outside of the boroughs of New York. Around this time GSH dropped "B Movie," which was an in-depth deconstruction of the election of Ronald Reagan and the negative implications that this would have on the nation as a whole. I remember hearing this on the radio when I was in high school, and even though I didn't know all the people in Reagan's cabinet or all the references that he made about "Ray Gun" that GSH tore apart, I quickly learned. Without knowing it, I had begun my own journey toward consciousness. It would take a few years to develop, but it was certainly set in place by listening to and learning this incredible song. How could I forget names like Caspar "the Defensive" Weinberger, George "Papa Doc" Bush, and "Attila" the Haig? GSH spoke volumes when he said that when America could no longer turn to John Wayne, it turned to Reagan, here again commenting on the importance that media icons played in helping to manipulate the masses. Public Enemy would famously pick up on this years later in "Fight the Power," when they said, "Elvis was a hero to most/but he never meant shit to me/ . . . muthafucka him and John Wayne!"

PHILADELPHIA INTERNATIONAL RECORDS

The success of Barry Gordy's Motown Records in Detroit starting in the '60s served as inspiration for two other Black record moguls out of Philadelphia in the '70s. Kenneth Gamble and Leon Huff started the Philadelphia International label in 1971, with backing from Columbia Records. Like Motown, Philly International had their own in-house band, known as MFSB, which officially stood for "Mother Father Sister Brother," but has also been rumored to have stood for "Mother Fuckin' Son of a Bitch." MFSB is best known for their instrumental single, "TSOP" (1974), which stood for "The Sound of Philadelphia," and is most widely recognized as the old theme song for *Soul Train*. Also, in-house writers like Gene McFadden and John Whitehead became famous for the popular 1979 anthem "Ain't No Stopping Us Now."

The Philly International label had a great deal of success during the 1970s as they began to redefine soul music in a way that proved so influential that their productions eventually served as the blueprint for the emergence of disco music in the mid- to late '70s. Lush string arrangements and thumping bass lines set the table for the disco revolution that was to come. Disco itself was wack, and I guess to some extent, Gamble and Huff could be held accountable for helping to create it, but it can't detract from the significance of the Philly International label at this time. The Philly sound came to be distinct, and even though they eventually faded, Gamble and Huff's output in the '70s must be recognized.

The two signature groups on this label were the O'Jays, led by Eddie Levert, and Harold Melvin and the Blue Notes.

The O'Jays, originally from Canton, Ohio, home of the NFL Hall of Fame, had several hits in the early '70s. "Back Stabbers" and "For the Love of Money" were two extremely popular songs that both had a cynical, though realistic, view of what was going on in America at the time. "Back Stabbers" could be said to be the precursor of the playa hater, a figure that would emerge years later in hip hop. The O'Jays talked about those who "smile in your face/all the time they wanna take your place," and took this a bit further in "For the Love of Money." In that song the O'Jays attacked the nature of greed circulating throughout the country, which was highlighted because of the Watergate scandal in Washington. Both of these songs would be used repeatedly in many television commercials and other forms of media over time, including the use of "For the Love of Money" as the theme song for the popular NBC reality show *The Apprentice* with Donald Trump.

The O'Jays also gained a lot of recognition from their popular single "Love Train," as well as a number of other hot cuts throughout the '70s. Eddie Levert's son, Gerald, would emerge in the '90s as a popular R & B singer in his own right.

Harold Melvin and the Blue Notes also made their mark during this time. Their success, however, was closely connected to the voice of their lead singer, Teddy Pendergrass. Although the group was named after Harold Melvin, it was Teddy who got all the recognition. The group scored hits with ballads like "If You Don't Know Me by Now," "The Love I Lost," and "I Hope That We Can Be Together Soon," which featured a moving duet between Teddy and Sharon Paige. But it was the more socially conscious lyrics of songs like "Bad Luck" and "Wake Up Everybody" that really highlighted Teddy's skills as a lead vocalist.

Following some internal conflicts with Melvin, Teddy decided to leave the group. Pendergrass began his solo career with the release of his self-titled debut album, *Teddy*, in 1977. Teddy was most similar to Marvin Gaye, since he had grown up in the

Black church and was an ordained minister as a young man. He, like Marvin, also began his career as a drummer. As Teddy evolved to stardom he became known for his sensual ballads, and Black women routinely saw him as a sex symbol. It seems that Teddy's star was rising as Marvin's was starting to momentarily decline in the late '70s.

Marvin had ushered in the sexually charged ballad with songs like "Let's Get It On," but by the time Teddy began to gain fame, the disco era, with all of its cocaine-fueled sexuality, was in full swing, and Teddy expanded on what Marvin had started. With songs like "Close the Door" and "Turn out the Lights," Teddy sounded like a preacher as he went about tryin' to get some draws. This merger of the sacred and sexual was again like Marvin, but this time with a deep baritone. Teddy got to be so popular with the ladies that he became known for his women-only concerts, at which the women in attendance were known to throw their panties on the stage. Teddy had become the biggest Black male sex symbol in a newly liberated world of Black sexuality. This came to define his career.

By the early '80s, Teddy, who would go on to release five platinum albums in a row, was on top of the world. He solidified this position when he released one of the best R & B songs, "Love TKO." It seemed that nothing could go wrong for Teddy Pendergrass. That changed in March 1982, when his Rolls-Royce crashed into a tree and he became paralyzed and confined to a wheelchair. Though he continued to record, his career was never the same after the accident. Teddy Pendergrass and Curtis Mayfield both experienced tragic accidents that brought sober ends to illustrious careers, but luckily we still have the music they created to remind us of their brilliance.

"BE THANKFUL FOR WHAT YOU GOT" (1974)

Many people may not recognize this song by its official name, but if they heard the hook "diamond in the back sunroof top/diggin' in the scene/with the gangster lean," it would no longer be a mystery. William DeVaughn's classic single, "Be Thankful for What You Got," which made it to number one on the R & B chart and number four on the pop chart, is one of those songs that has the Super Fly '70s written all over it.

DeVaughn, the Washington, DC, native and certified one-hit wonder, was most certainly bitin' Curtis Mayfield's distinct falsetto style on his hit song. MFSB provided the laid-back groove of this classic. The addictive hook of "Be Thankful" also became a catchphrase in its own right during this time.

What I have always found most interesting about this single is that it has long been assumed that the song was an anthem to the pimp life, though it's really just the opposite. The celebration of a "fat-ass hog," also known as a Cadillac Eldorado, with a diamond-shaped vinyl covering on the back window and a sunroof top, backed by the slow groove of the song, suggested "the life" and all its attendant pleasures. But if you pay close attention to the lyrics, they reveal that the song was really a critique of the ubiquitous consumption that had started to define life in the inner city. DeVaughn's suggestion that even though "you may not have a car at all" but "you can still stand tall" is evidence of the fact that he was dissin' the materialism inherent in the life as opposed to simply celebrating it. Thus, "Be Thankful for What You Got," as opposed to coveting something—a car, a lifestyle—that you do not have. But the hook and the overall groove of the song were so equally smooth and catchy that people just locked in on those things and didn't really pay attention to what the lyrics actually said. This is not unlike the reaction to Bruce Springsteen's classic "Born in the USA" in the 1980s, which was a critique of American dominance and imperialism, though many thought that it was an anthem.

"Be Thankful for What You Got" helps to define the Super Fly '70s through its chill, weed-induced, pimped-out sound, and its evocation of images from the pimp life, in spite of the inherent critique in the lyrics. The song indeed sounds and feels like the '70s, and for me this song, maybe more than any other single, embodies the essence of the Super Fly '70s in no uncertain terms.

"SMILING FACES SOMETIMES" (1971)

This is one of my favorite singles of all time. Motown producer Norman Whitfield, who was especially noted for his work with the Temptations, put together the vocal trio the Undisputed Truth. The band included Joe Harris, the lead singer, along with Billie Rae Calvin and Brenda Joyce, who appeared onstage wearing white facepaint and huge silver Afro wigs, a style that evoked early funkadelic. Whitfield used the Undisputed Truth as an opportunity to try out his "psychedelic soul" concept. The producer was known for recording the same songs with different groups, and there were several songs that went back and forth between the Undisputed Truth and the more popular Temptations.

The only big hit for the Undisputed Truth was their 1971 recording of the song "Smiling Faces Sometimes," a track originally released by the Temptations in the same year. The Undisputed Truth's version of the song reached as high as number three on the pop charts. The Temptations' version used a score similar to that of a horror film, and most of the original twelve-minute recording was an extended instrumental riff with no vocals, while the Undisputed Truth's version dropped the extended instrumental and focused more on the sound interplay and contrasts between Harris's lead vocals and his female background singers, Calvin and Joyce.

In 1971, the Undisputed Truth had originally recorded the song "Papa Was a Rolling Stone," which the Temptations remade into a number one pop hit in 1972. The Temptations eventually won three Grammy awards for the song in 1973.

The point of the song "Smiling Faces" is that "sometimes they don't tell the truth/smiling faces/tell lies and I got proof." It goes on to say, "Beware of the handshake and the pat on the back." In other words, watch your back.

"Smiling Faces Sometimes" is quite similar to the O'Jays classic hit "Back Stabbers," which was released in 1972. One can only imagine that these songs were in response to the suspicions among many in the African American community regarding the supposedly liberal attitudes toward race that had come about as a result of the civil rights and Black power movements.

PART

4

Whatcha See Is Whatcha Get

TV AND SPORTS ICONS OF THE SUPER FLY '70S

newly minted sense of Black expression could also be seen on television in the Super Fly '70s, though to a somewhat lesser extent than was the case in film and music. Nonetheless, when combining all of these areas of culture, it was as though a Black wave of entertainment were now overtaking the nation. For instance, *The Flip Wilson Show* debuted on NBC in 1970, a variety show in which comedian Flip Wilson exposed the nation to his own comedic style, especially his characters Reverend Leroy, the jackleg preacher who headed "the Church of What's Happenin' Now," and Flip's most famous character, Geraldine, which featured Flip in drag playing the sexy, sassy sista who became the model for both Martin Lawrence's Shanaynay and Jamie Foxx's Ugly Wanda in the '90s.

Richard Pryor, the man whose comedy albums set the standard, and the cat who in my mind was really the voice of the '70s, also had a short-lived variety show in 1977 entitled *The Richard*

Pryor Show—but the show was canceled after four shows due to conflicts with NBC over the comedian's controversial material.

Comedian Bill Cosby, who made history as the first African American to have a lead role in a television series, costarring with Robert Culp in *I Spy* (1965–68), had an impact on the Saturday-morning network lineup with his animated series *Fat Albert and the Cosby Kids* that debuted in 1972. *Fat Albert*, with Cosby doing the voices for the characters, revolved around stories of the comedian's life in Philly growing up around a group of 'hood friends, many of whom, quite ironically, could be said to resemble the dysfunctional urban Black people whom Cosby repeatedly dissed in a series of public speeches in recent years.

What I always liked about *Fat Albert*, though, was the way the characters would sing a song at the end of each episode, distilling the moral lesson of the day's show into a corny-ass musical number that proved hard to forget. There was something about being a young Black kid and seeing other Black kids animated on a Saturday-morning show that still hits home for me, in spite of my many disagreements with Cosby's current old-school playa hatin'.

Television in the late '60s and early '70s had begun to feature more Black actors in significant roles. However, a sustained Black presence in genres other than the sitcom proved somewhat elusive. Actors like Cosby in *I Spy* and also as the high school coach Chet Kincaid in *The Bill Cosby Show* (1969–71), along with Diahann Carroll, who represented a positive image starring as the middle-class nurse and single mother in the show *Julia* in 1968, had certainly made an impact—but these shows were off the air by 1971.

There were also Black actors like Greg Morris in *Mission Impossible* (1966–73), Denise Nicholas and Lloyd Haynes in *Room 222* (1969–74), and Clarence Williams III in *The Mod Squad* (1968–73), who were prominently featured in their respective shows as well. In addition, there were crime shows based on the movie *Shaft* (1973–74) and *Tenafly* starring James McEachin—created by Richard Levinson and William Link, the pair behind the ever-popular *Columbo* series starring Peter Falk—about a Black private detective, which debuted as a made-for-television movie in 1973 and returned with four more episodes over the next year.

Two made-for-television movies drew a lot of ratings and attention during this time. One of these was *Brian's Song* (1971), about the life of Chicago Bears running back Brian Piccolo and his struggle with cancer, which costarred Billy Dee Williams as Piccolo's teammate and friend Gale Sayers. The other was *The Autobiography of Miss Jane Pittman* (1974), based on Ernest Gaines's novel, which starred Cicely Tyson in the lead role.

Beginning in 1972, though, with *Sanford and Son*, which was followed by *Good Times* in 1974 and *The Jeffersons* in 1975, the entire nation soon found itself glued to these popular crossover sitcoms about Black life. Other, less popular, though significant Black sitcoms, like *That's My Momma* (1974–75) and *What's Happening?* (1976–79)—which was also created by Eric Monte, the writer of *Cooley High* and cocreator of *Good Times*—made it seem as though we had gone from lack to abundance overnight.

The images ranged from Chicago's Cabrini-Green housing projects on *Good Times*, moving on up to the "de-luxe apartment in the sky" of *The Jeffersons*, with the Watts junkyard of *Sanford*

and Son somewhere in between. Though these shows couldn't always escape the stereotypical, they provided a recurring series of images that will forever serve as a glimpse of Blackness whenever one thinks about the decade of the '70s.

One of the biggest events of '70s television was, without a doubt, the premiere of the miniseries *Roots: The Saga of an American Family* on ABC over eight nights in 1977. The miniseries featured a long list of Black actors, many of whom got their first major exposure because of *Roots*. These actors include John Amos, Cicely Tyson, Leslie Uggams, future Academy Award winner Lou Gossett Jr., Richard Roundtree, Ben Vereen, and the now-disgraced former NFL great O. J. Simpson, among others. Even celebrated author, poet, and overall cultural figure Dr. Maya Angelou appeared in the miniseries.

Based on the best-selling novel of the same name by author Alex Haley—who had also cowritten *The Autobiography of Malcolm X—Roots* tells the story of several generations of Haley's own family. Haley won both a Pulitzer Prize and a National Book Award for his work, and the book spent nine months on the *New York Times* best-seller list.

The television miniseries began with the capture in Africa of Kunta Kinte, played by newcomer LeVar Burton, continued through the torturous Middle Passage, all the way over to America, where Kunta would be enslaved, and began the odyssey that represented life in this nation for the slaves and their descendants. This was the first time that the "peculiar institution" known as slavery would be dramatized on TV for American audiences, and the impact would be phenomenal.

Roots is said to have attracted somewhere in the neighborhood of 130 million viewers over the course of its eight-night run, and the series finale is still considered the third-most-watched television program ever. The miniseries won nine Emmys as well as a Peabody Award. The huge crossover success exposed slavery for what it was, to many Americans who had no idea of how indebted this nation was to the slaves and their descendants, while also making popular a search for one's own "roots," which created a strong interest in genealogical research for people of all races.

Roots also assisted in giving Black people a better sense of their own heritage and spurred notions of Afrocentric thought in various segments of the community. It is said that many Black families named their daughters "Kizzy," after the Leslie Uggams character in the miniseries, just one example of the program's influence.

In 1979, ABC broadcast *Roots: The Next Generation*, a second fourteen-hour sequel to the original, and this series brought the story up to the present day.

I should also point out that Haley's book enjoyed its share of controversy over the years as well. Many have even accused Haley of plagiarism. Alex Haley was sued by author Harold Courlander and his publisher, who claimed that Haley had plagiarized from his 1968 book *The African*. According to "Uncovering *Roots*," a *Village Voice* retrospective article written in February 1993, Haley, desperate to finish his book, had threaded eighty or so passages from *The African* throughout *Roots*. Haley reached a settlement with Courlander and Crown Publishers for $650,000 in December 1978. In cross-examination, Haley even admitted to appropriating from a seventeenth-century West

African travelogue called *The Travels of Mungo Park* and Shirley Graham's *The Story of Phyllis Wheatley*, a biography about a young female slave, in order to fill pages. Haley was also sued by Margaret Walker, who charged that he had lifted from her book *Jubilee* as well, but this case was dismissed by the courts. All in all, Haley's work in *Roots* was eventually labeled with the term *faction,* alluding to its willful merger of fact and fiction, but this in no way takes away from the impact that the book and, more important, the television miniseries had on America.

One cannot begin to imagine a television event having such an impact now or at any time in the future as *Roots* did in the '70s. This program probably did more to expose America's slave past and the lasting impact that this institution has on our society, however "factional" it may have been, than any class, history textbook, or other more formal treatment of the subject matter. *Roots* demonstrated that Black history was indeed American history, and, by turning this into a pop cultural moment on television, it was able to influence the way that society thought about the lingering issue of race in this country, for better or for worse. One can never underestimate the influence that this strong showing had on defining the Super Fly '70s.

DIDN'T I BLOW YOUR MIND THIS TIME?
BLACK ATHLETES CHANGE THE GAME

One of the other areas of the culture where you could increasingly see Black icons on television was in the realm of sports.

Starting in the late '60s, as more and more Black athletes were allowed to attend major universities, the professional leagues began seeing increasing numbers of Black athletes in their respective sports.

In addition to the athletes themselves, sports demonstrated a uniquely Black style of competition in the process. Clearly, sports meant more to these Black athletes than it did for others, because this was a way to demonstrate through competition a certain dominance. Such opportunities were seldom available to Blacks in other parts of society. These successful athletes brought their own cultural style to bear on the games as well.

Take, for example, the increasing visibility of the end zone dance after a touchdown in football. Elmo Wright, a receiver for the Kansas City Chiefs, is credited with doing the first end zone dance in a game against the Houston Oilers on November 13, 1973. Wright's high-steppin' moves were only the tip of the iceberg, though. The Houston Oilers' Billy "White Shoes" Johnson, the man who made the touchdown dance famous in the '70s, often looked like he was on *Soul Train* after he scored, with dance moves that would have made everyone at the popular Studio 54 take notice. White Shoes, whose main dance was a version of the popular "funky chicken," with the ball held high over his head, was not alone, though, as numerous other NFL players, like the Lions' David Hill, for instance, got their groove on after scoring a touchdown. It got to the point where people often wanted to see the dances more than the actual touchdown or the game itself. There were many people in the media, league office, and at home watching on television who hated this aspect of the game, but this only made it that much more enjoyable for all of those who wanted to see a little entertainment added to the proceed-ings. The end zone dance is now an NFL staple, and many play-ers over the years have added their names to the list that was started by Wright and White Shoes back in the day. There were "the Smurfs," a group of players from the Washington Redskins in the '80s, Deion "Prime Time" Sanders in the '90s, and modern players like Ray Lewis, Chad Johnson, Joe Horn, and Terrell "T. O." Owens, who continue the tradition in an especially styl-ized and, at times, over-the-top fashion to this day.

The place where you could see the biggest impact of Black culture in sports was on the basketball court. The '70s is the point at which the game of basketball started to become the sport of choice for young Black men, especially those in urban areas. In the early '70s, native Detroiter Spencer Haywood was the first player to declare himself a "hardship" case in successfully chal-lenging the eligibility requirement in professional basketball. The rule said that a player's college class had to have graduated before he could declare himself eligible for the NBA draft. Hay-wood started a trend of great college players who left their uni-versities early to pursue a career in the NBA, which eventually led to younger high school players deciding to skip college alto-gether and go straight to the pros. (As of 2006–07, players will have to be a minimum of nineteen years old before they are eli-gible for the draft.)

By the late '60s one could see glimpses of the way that many players would begin incorporating the styles of street ball into their professional repertoire. Philly native and star of both the Baltimore Bullets and the New York Knicks Earl "the Pearl" Monroe (once known as "Black Jesus" in Philly on the playgrounds of the City of Brotherly Love) was as smooth as they come with his ice-cold court game. The NBA, however, was facing competition from an upstart league, the ABA, and in this league players were allowed more freedom in how they played their game as opposed to the more conservative style of NBA basketball.

The ABA featured players like Julius "Dr. J" Erving, David "Skywalker" Thompson, and George "the Iceman" Gervin, all of whom brought their own unique interpretation of street-ball style into the game at a professional level. These men became icons of their times for making the game as much an artistic display as it was athletic. This style eventually came to the NBA when the ABA folded and the NBA took in four of the teams that had originally been in the ABA.

By the mid-70s, the dunk became a signature shot for a lot of players, as well as a great vehicle for self-expression. Guys like Dr. J and Skywalker were both known for their incredible ability to dunk the basketball with style and flair. Again, many disliked the shot, but the streets loved it, and it is now an integral part of any basketball game. The Iceman was known for his ability to "finger roll," and this too was emblematic of the best street ball traditions. Top it all off with some of the slickest dressers, like Walt "Clyde" Frazier, and some of the baddest Afros you've ever seen, like that of Indiana's Darnell Hillman, and you get the picture. Professional basketball was a stage for a unique style, straight from the streets of urban America.

Then there were the individual sports, like boxing. Muhammad Ali represented a triumph of the human spirit in his battles, both in the court of law and in his attempt to regain the heavyweight championship of the world after having his title stripped for refusing to enlist in the Vietnam War in 1967. Ali prevailed in the Supreme Court in 1971, and he went on to regain his title with a dramatic victory over George Foreman in 1975. In the sport of tennis, a bespectacled Arthur Ashe shocked the world when he defeated Jimmy Conners to win Wimbledon in 1975 by outsmarting him at a time when it was still thought that Black athletes were perhaps superior physically, but inferior in terms of their ability to use their minds. Ashe's dominance of what was an all-White sport at the time certainly helped pave the way for Serena and Venus Williams's success on the tennis courts in the modern era. Black athletes and their phenomenal success in athletic pursuits, along with their distinct style of execution, made sports an integral part of the overall vibe of the era.

Check it out: What follows are some words of wisdom on *Sanford and Son, Good Times,* and *Soul Train.* But don't change that channel—you knew I couldn't end this without showing love to some of the coldest cats ever to do it. Read about how Muhammad Ali became the greatest of all time, how a dude like Dr. J became an icon, how Hank Aaron broke the most cherished record in baseball, how Black athletes moved from the playing field to Hollywood, and how a cat like Darryl Dawkins came down from Planet Lovetron to bless us all with broken backboards and wild-ass ways.

SANFORD AND SON (1972–77)

The Super Fly '70s were not just relegated to film and music. With the launch of *Sanford and Son* as a midseason replacement on the NBC network in 1972, television became another venue for the expression of Black culture. *Sanford and Son* was the brainchild of producer Norman Lear, who seemed to have television in the palm of his hand in the early '70s. He created *All in the Family*, *Maude*, *Good Times*, and *The Jeffersons*, with each program offering some take on the prevalent social issues of the day, especially the issue of race. These socially inclined programs were a hallmark of the early '70s, and the shows, all of which featured Black performers, were both popular and controversial.

Sanford and Son revolved around the exploits of Fred Sanford, a Watts junkman, played by comedian Redd Foxx. Fred lived with his son, Lamont, played by Demond Wilson. Elizabeth, Fred's wife and Lamont's mother, has passed away, so father and son often act like a married couple. Whenever Fred encounters a stressful situation he will put his hand over his heart and declare, "Elizabeth, I'm coming to join you, honey!"

Redd Foxx was a popular Black comedian on the famed chitlin circuit, a loose collection of theaters around the country that catered to Black audiences when America was still segregated by race. Foxx originally began recording what were called blue records in the 1950s. Blue records were adult records that used language and discussed issues that were considered to be

vulgar and profane. Many record stores would stock these records only under the counter or at the back of the record bins, hidden completely out of sight, as they were quite scandalous in their day. Because Foxx's material was considered too offensive for mainstream White tastes in the '50s and early '60s, he was relegated to doing nightclub shows and did not experience the widespread success that someone like Bill Cosby was beginning to enjoy at the time. For this reason, Foxx was able to maintain his edge without having to compromise for a mainstream audience, at least not until he appeared on *Sanford and Son*.

GOOD TIMES (1974–79)

One of several popular Black sitcoms of the '70s, *Good Times* was set around the Evans family, who lived in a high-rise housing project in Chicago similar to the notorious real-life Cabrini-Green and Robert Taylor projects. The father, James Evans, was played by actor John Amos, while the mother, Florida, was played by Esther Rolle; the children included daughter Thelma (BernNadette Stanis), and sons Michael (Ralph Carter) and—the character who would become the focus of the show—J.J., played by comedian Jimmie Walker.

This was another of producer Norman Lear's many successful television shows in the '70s. *Good Times* was actually a spinoff of the show *Maude*, the Bea Arthur star vehicle that ran from 1972–78, in which Florida had been Maude's maid. *Maude* had been a spinoff of the ever-popular *All in the Family* (1971–79). Lear was also responsible for both *Sanford and Son* (1972–77) and *The Jeffersons* (1975–85) two other Black sitcoms of the period that all at one point ranked in the top ten of the Nielsen ratings.

Lear's work was known for examining the social issues of the day through comedy, and *Good Times* was no different, though looking back on it now, Lear helped to perpetuate an image of poor Black people who were stuck in the 'hood and couldn't manage to get out. What made this even worse was the fact that the show would start to focus more attention on the J.J. character, whose buffoonish, Stepin Fetchit–like disposition and repeated utterance of his signature line "Dy-no-mite!" made him a huge favorite with some fans, but led to dissension in the show's cast. Both Esther Rolle and John Amos were pissed that the show was moving away from focusing on the parents and the plight of the Black family. Instead, the show increasingly highlighted J.J.'s outlandish antics. Amos was dismissed from the cast in 1976 when it was time to renew his contract and written off as having died in a

car accident, prompting a reference years later in an episode of Martin Lawrence's sitcom, *Martin*, in the '90s, and also serving as inspiration for the hook of the Outkast song "Spottie-OttieDopaliscious" from their '98 album *Aquemini*. After making some very pointed and critical comments about the direction that the show was going in, Esther Rolle left *Good Times* for a short time, but later returned. Another interesting point about the show's politics was that Michael, the youngest child in the family, was the character who spouted off Black power political ideas that were played for jokes because they came out of the mouth of the "militant midget" as opposed to one of the adult characters.

All of this notwithstanding, *Good Times* does provide some fond memories of at least seeing Black life on screen, however limited the representation might have been at the time. *Good Times*, like the Diahann Carroll and James Earl Jones film *Claudine*, attempted to deal with the issues facing a poor Black family, and offered a somewhat different twist on the times than was the case with so many of the other urban-themed, crime-specific images of that time. The thing about the Super Fly '70s is that before this era, there was virtually no Black representation at all on television, but by the '70s this representation proved to be some of the most popular around.

One of the things that stands out about *Good Times* is the addition to the cast of Penny, played by a young Janet Jackson. Penny was adopted by the Evans's neighbor Willona, who was played by Ja'net DuBois, who herself sang the theme song to *The Jeffersons*. Penny was a victim of child abuse at the hands of her mother, played by Chip Fields, the real-life mother of Kim Fields, the actress who came to fame for her role as Tootie on the '80s TV show *The Facts of Life*. The role on *Good Times* introduced Janet Jackson to the American public as another one of the talented Jackson Five clan, and she would go on to have her own highly successful recording career, along with a few roles here and there on both the big and small screens.

SOUL TRAIN (1971–PRESENT)

There was probably no better barometer of what was hot in the Super Fly '70s than the syndicated Black musical and cultural showcase *Soul Train*. "The hippest trip in America," as it was described, featured the top soul artists of the day lip-synching their hits in front of a live group of dancers who showed off the latest moves and the coolest fashions of the day. *Soul Train* featured real

people doing real dances and wearing the ultimate in fly gear for a syndicated audience that stretched across the nation. If you wanted to be cool and down with what was really going on, then *Soul Train* was your destination every Saturday.

The show's creator and host for twenty-three years was the baritone-voiced Don Cornelius, who was known for wishing you "love, peace, and soul" at the end of every episode. The show got its start on a Chicago UHF station with an investment from Sears, Roebuck and Co. in 1970, and was syndicated nationally in 1971. The guests on the first nationally syndicated show were Gladys Knight and the Pips, Eddie Kendricks, Honey Cone, and Bobby Hutton.

This syndication deal meant that for people who didn't live in the most urban of areas, there was still hope, as *Soul Train* was able to provide a glimpse into the hottest trends and latest dances for anyone who had the privilege of seeing the show. For many suburbanites, the show offered a look from a distance into contemporary Black culture without their having to leave their living rooms.

Soul Train was primarily underwritten by the advertising dollars of Black business pioneer John H. Johnson, publisher of *Ebony* and *Jet* magazines and owner of Johnson Products, who were the "makers of Ultra Sheen, Afro Sheen, and Ultra Sheen cosmetics," as the familiar voice would intone during each episode. This was a marriage made in heaven, as it wouldn't be hard to imagine that Johnson would have had an extremely difficult time getting advertising time on White television programs, and Cornelius would have had difficulty attracting enough White advertisers to support a show like *Soul Train*, considering the racial politics of the 1970s.

The show's familiar theme song was "The Sound of Philadelphia (TSOP)," performed by the group MSFB, and some of the regular features of the show were the Soul Train Scrabble Board, where dancers attempted to unscramble the names of famous Black people, and the Soul Train Line, a dance showcase where male and female couples got their groove on as they moved down the line, one after the other. The Soul Train Line even became a staple at Black parties, weddings, and other social functions due to the popularity of this show.

Though *Soul Train* was primarily focused on soul music, several White artists also appeared on the show over the years, starting with Elton John's appearance when he performed "Bennie and the Jets" in 1974. There is not a Black artist of note you can name who didn't appear on the show at one time or another.

By the '80s, as music videos started to dominate the representation of music on television, and a cable channel like BET came to the fore, the function and purpose of *Soul Train* began to change. The show could no longer lay claim to offering the only consistent venue where one could see these types of acts and hear Black music. The show, though still on the air, has suffered ever since these changes came about. Nevertheless, you cannot sleep on the importance of *Soul Train* to the overall image of the Super Fly '70s.

MUHAMMAD ALI

What can you say about the man formerly known as Cassius Marcellus Clay that hasn't been said already? There are few icons of any era or from any other walk of life more recognized now than Ali was and is. Ali had won the heavyweight title in 1964 with a dramatic victory over the ex-con Sonny Liston. When he refused to be drafted to fight the war in Vietnam in 1967, he not only transcended the world of boxing, but he also permanently etched his name in the annals of Americana. When he made his miraculous comeback to championship form in 1975, he became the most important American athlete ever. We know all of this now, but back in the '70s, people were not nearly as enamored of him as they have become over time, especially since he lit the torch at the 1996 Olympics in Atlanta. There, he experienced a rebirth that continues to live on until this day and will certainly define him from now on.

Though it was in 1964 when Ali originally won the title, it

was in the Super Fly '70s that he really made his mark in the ring with one of the greatest comeback stories ever. Having been banned from boxing and having had his title stripped away from him after his refusal to be drafted, he was not allowed to travel, and, in effect, not able to really make a living.

Ali returned to the ring in 1970 against Jerry Quarry in Atlanta, Georgia—a state where it was somewhat easier to navigate the legal terrain regarding his status because Georgia did not have a boxing commission. In his return, Ali found himself deeply influenced by the plight and legacy of another Black boxer who had encountered the wrath of the government and the White public at an earlier time, a man who was being reconsidered along the new political lines of Black consciousness prevalent in the early '70s. This man was none other than Jack Johnson.

From Ali's corner during the night of the Quarry fight, Ali's hype man, Drew "Bundini" Brown, is reported to have repeatedly yelled, "Ghost in the house. Ghost in the house. Jack Johnson's here. Ghost in the house," as a form of encouragement to his fighter. The "ghost" that Bundini was referring to, the great Jack Johnson, was the first Black man ever to win the heavyweight title back in 1908.

Jack Johnson was quite a controversial figure in his time. He was unapologetically brash, quite flamboyant in his style as well as in his lack of humility toward the White establishment. Among other things, Jack Johnson openly flaunted his relationship with White women at a time when a Black person could get lynched for even thinking about looking in a White woman's direction.

As the civil rights movement gave way to the Black power movement, there was a concerted effort among conscientious

Black people to find historical figures who reflected the struggles of their times but were relevant as examples in that present moment also. This is the role that Jack Johnson filled for Ali, especially in light of Ali's struggles over his refusal to go to Vietnam and the government's intervention in his quest to make a living.

In the late '60s and early '70s, Jack Johnson was discovered by a new generation. In December 1967, playwright Howard Sackler staged *The Great White Hope*, a fictional play based on a character named Jack Jefferson. This character was obviously patterned after Johnson and was played by actor James Earl Jones. In 1968, the play won a Tony Award, a New York Drama Critics' Circle Award, and the Pulitzer Prize. Released as a film in 1970, with Jones still in the lead role, *The Great White Hope* went on to earn Academy Award nominations for Jones as well as his costar, Jane Alexander. In 1971 Miles Davis released the album *A Tribute to Jack Johnson*, which was the music he had recorded for the sound track of the documentary *Jack Johnson* (1970), produced by Bill Cayton (who would later emerge as one of Mike Tyson's managers). The documentary would also be nominated for Best Documentary at the Academy Awards. This was only the first resurrection of Johnson's image, though, as the Ken Burns–produced *Unforgivable Blackness* debuted on PBS in 2005, featuring music by Wynton Marsalis. The mythic image of the rebel outlaw Johnson, a Black man who didn't give a fuck, was certainly the kind of image and legacy that Ali wanted to be linked with upon his return to the ring in the early '70s.

By 1971 sentiment in America against the war had increased dramatically from what it had been in 1967, and Ali won a Supreme Court decision that overturned his original conviction.

Ali fought the first of three matches against his archrival, Smokin' Joe Frazier, in New York's Madison Square Garden in 1971. Frazier defeated Ali, even knocking him down in the final round, in what will forever live on as one of the all-time greatest fights. Ali suffered a broken jaw in a loss to Ken Norton in 1973 as well before he was granted the opportunity to fight the behemoth George Foreman in a 1975 Zaire bout dubbed "The Rumble in the Jungle." This fight has been immortalized in the excellent documentary *When We Were Kings*.

Ali's effective use of the rope-a-dope strategy against a much bigger, stronger, and more menacing Foreman worked to lure Big George into a trap as Ali lay on the ropes in the early rounds and let Foreman fire away on him. Foreman eventually got tired, and then Ali jumped in for the kill, knocking Foreman out and regaining his title. This was probably the greatest upset in the history of sports. Many people feared that Ali was so overmatched against Foreman that he risked losing his life, so his unexpected triumph was that much sweeter when it went down.

In 1975 Ali would fight Frazier for the third and final time in what many have dubbed the greatest fight ever. This was, of course, known as the Thriller in Manila. Ali defeated Smokin' Joe and probably should have retired after such an incredible run, but he kept coming back for more. Many medical experts have concluded that too many blows to the head proved to be a strong contributing factor to Ali's developing Parkinson's disease in his later years. Ali did have one final triumph, though, when he defeated Leon Spinks in a 1978 rematch to regain his title for the third time.

Ali will forever live as the spirit of the Super Fly '70s for his refusal to be taken down by the forces that were aligned against him. Most interesting, though, is the fact that of the many people who have embraced him in the present, some of these same people have no idea what he went through back in the day. Now he is often celebrated and held high by culture as a whole, but there was a time when Ali was a very divisive figure and only his die-hard supporters had love for him. As such, a lot of this recent admiration is less compelling to me, because I remember when I was comin' up that there were people who hated him as much as the public seems to love him now. Ali starred in movies like *The Greatest* (1977), acted on Broadway in the play *Buck White*, and even fought to a draw a Japanese wrestler named Antonio Inoki. He did it all. His defiance, his spirit, and his incredible gifts in the ring will forever define him as one who has no peers.

JULIUS "DR. J" ERVING

I would not be the Notorious Ph.D. today if it were not for the man known as Dr. J back in the Super Fly '70s. I had an intense desire to be called Doctor, but there was no way in hell I was going to ever qualify to be a medical doctor. It didn't matter anyway; I wanted a Ph.D., and I most definitely wanted to be called Dr. Boyd or Dr. B, all because of Dr. J.

There is no more of an appropriate icon from the era than Dr. J. His Afro Sheen blowout-kit 'fro, the knee pads, the Converse Dr. J's, and, of course, his graceful ability to glide through the air with that red-white-and-blue ABA (American Basketball

Association) ball looking like it was an extension of his outstretched hand—this is an image that will never be forgotten. Doc was the Super Fly '70s in no uncertain terms.

Julius Erving, a native of Roosevelt, Long Island, played two years of college basketball at the University of Massachusetts before joining the fledging Virginia Squires of the American Basketball Association in 1971. In 1973, Doc was traded to the New York Nets. This is where he would start to get his reputation as the most exciting player in the game.

Dr. J is the player who made the dunk shot an integral part of the game, and he is also the player who brought the street game into professional basketball. His penchant for high-flying style was straight off the blacktop. Doc played the game above the rim, and he, along with other players, like Elgin Baylor, Connie Hawkins, and Doc's contemporary David "Skywalker" Thompson, made this style of play common. In so doing, they set the table for the emergence of Michael Jordan.

In 1976, Doc and the Skywalker faced off in the ABA slam-dunk competition. This was the greatest dunk competition ever, though Jordan and Dominique Wilkins had some great slam battles in the '80s. Doc won the competition, though Skywalker was a more than worthy opponent. The dunk that won it all for Doc was one where he jumped from the free throw line and threw down a monstrous slam and had everyone in attendance standing with their mouths wide open. This dunk was so incredible that Jordan would later copy it, though adding his own unique twist.

The ABA folded the same year, and Doc ended up going to the NBA and playing for the Philadelphia 76ers. Between 1977 and 1983, Doc's team made the NBA finals four times, with him finally winning his one and only championship ring in '83. This was the season when 76er center Moses Malone made his famous prediction that Philly would walk through the play-offs and the finals, taking each series "fo' fo' fo'," which, translated, meant that they would dominate with a four-game sweep in each round. The actual results were four, five, four, but it didn't matter; Moses wasn't far off in predicting Philly's dominance.

Dr. J retired from the NBA in 1987, and in his final season he enjoyed celebrations of his career at every arena in the league. In spite of all his success with the 76ers in the '80s, Doc will forever be an icon of the Super Fly '70s.

HANK AARON

One of my earliest sports memories takes me back to April 8, 1974. This was the night that "the Hammer," Hank Aaron of the Atlanta Braves, broke Babe Ruth's celebrated Major League Baseball home run record when he hit his 715th career homer off of the Dodgers' Al Downing in the Atlanta Stadium. I have now seen the image of Hank rounding those bases what seems like a million times, but the joy of that moment is the same no matter how many times I've seen it before. What I remember most is seeing these two White cats seemingly emerge out of nowhere as they came running toward Hank—who was looking somewhat suspiciously at them as they got closer—only to finally accept the hands of congratulations that they were extending in his direction.

Watching Hank round those bases was like watching a

marathon runner approach the finish line victorious, and as I got older what I learned was that Hank had indeed been running a marathon of his own, and that his 715th home run was a fitting culmination.

The game of baseball has always been a celebrated sport in America. It was the American pastime, after all. The legends of the sport, the records, the lore—this is all part of American history and identity. So is the fact that up until 1947, Black players couldn't even play in the league. The breaking of the color line in baseball is also a well-known moment, and Jackie Robinson, the person who broke it, has become a significant figure himself in the history of American society for this very reason.

The home run record, the most cherished record in the sport, was now being broken by a Black man only twenty-seven short years after the game was initially integrated in 1947. And not only was it just the record itself, but it was the fact that the record belonged to the man who is considered the greatest player in the history of the game, the Bambino, Babe Ruth. Hank was breaking a record, and he was really rewriting the history of the sport at the same time.

The history behind Hank Aaron—a native of Mobile, Alabama, who is currently a front-office executive with the Braves—breaking Babe's record is interesting in and of itself. There were a lot of White fans who did not want to see the record broken, and there were some racists who had been sending Hank death threats, saying that if he broke the record they would take his life. The hate mail and just straight-up hatin' in general that he received in his quest to break the record made it that much more important. I'm sure that when Hank saw those two guys running in his direction, the thought crossed his mind that perhaps these were people sent to kill him.

To complicate matters, Hank had received a lot of negativity from the Major League Baseball front office. Hank had ended the 1973 season needing only two home runs to break the record, so at the beginning of 1974 it was thought that he might eclipse Ruth in the Atlanta Braves' opening road series against the Cincinnati Reds. But Hank wanted to accomplish this feat at home in Atlanta, so he was going to sit out the Reds series— until baseball commissioner Bowie Kuhn ordered him to play. Hank asked Kuhn if he would have a moment of silence before the game played on April 4, 1974, in honor of the sixth anniversary of the assassination of Dr. Martin Luther King Jr. Kuhn refused. Not only was Hank being ordered to play by the league offices, but it was insult added to injury when his simple request to respect the memory of Dr. King was not honored either. Overcoming all of this made the moment that he actually broke the record that much sweeter.

BLACK ATHLETES IN HOLLYWOOD

With the sudden popularity of blaxploitation films in the '70s, Hollywood found itself in need of acting talent to fulfill the roles of this burgeoning genre. Because there had been so few Black films and limited roles for Black actors in Hollywood before this time, there was no ready pool of talent to draw from. But Hollywood was not going to let this trend pass, so they went out to find

Black actors wherever they could. Tamara Dobson of *Cleopatra Jones* fame had originally been a model, and Gloria Hendry, who in 1973 alone appeared in *Black Caesar, Hell Up in Harlem*, and as the first Black woman to be romantically involved with James Bond in *Live and Let Die*, had been a Playboy Bunny. Yet there was no other area of the culture at large that seemed to provide more new actors than that of the sports world, where Hollywood hoped to capitalize on the name recognition that these individuals had achieved in their respective sports.

The move from the athletic playing field to the big screen for Black actors can be traced back to someone like Woody Strode, a former all-American at UCLA and one of the first African Americans to play in the National Football League. He appeared in many films dating back to the 1940s through the 1990s, including *The Ten Commandments* (1956) and his most famous role as Draba in the Stanley Kubrick film *Spartacus* (1960), where he engages in a fierce battle with the film's star, Kirk Douglas.

In the early 1960s, Jim Brown of the Cleveland Browns was without question the best player in professional football. He was cast in the film *The Dirty Dozen*, which was released in 1967, but Brown was still working on the film in July of 1966 when Cleveland owner Art Modell insisted that he return from London, where the film was being shot, to report to training camp. When the two could not work out their differences, Brown announced his retirement on July 14, 1966, and went into acting full-time.

Brown, who brought his tough-as-nails, strong-Black-man persona with him to the screen from the gridiron, went on to star in several films, including *Ice Station Zebra* (1968), *100 Rifles* (1969), in which he had a historic interracial sex scene with

White actress Raquel Welch, and . . . *tick* . . . *tick* . . . *tick* . . .
(1970), before moving on to starring roles in blaxploitation films
like *Slaughter, Slaughter's Big Rip-Off*, and the classic *Three the
Hard Way*. For a time in the late '60s and early '70s, many specu-
lated that Brown was on his way to becoming a harder version of
screen star Sidney Poitier, but as the blaxploitation era dwindled,
Brown's star seemed to descend as well, though his name has
never been forgotten.

Jim Brown was the head of his friend Richard Pryor's production company, Indigo Films, in the early 1980s before being fired
by Pryor over "creative differences." The former football great has
continued to appear in films, including a role in the blaxploitation parody *I'm Gonna Git You Sucka*, and a reunion of blaxploitation stars Richard Roundtree, Ron O'Neal, Fred Williamson, and
Pam Grier in *Original Gangstas* (1996). Over the years he has had
many run-ins with the law, several of which resulted from allega-
tions of domestic violence. He has gained frequent media attention for criticizing contemporary Black athletes like Michael
Jordan and Tiger Woods for their lack of consciousness and political involvement. Brown has long been involved in community
activism, starting the Negro Industrial and Economic Union
while still in Cleveland in the 1960s, and serving as the vice president of the Hollywood/Beverly Hills chapter of the NAACP in
the '70s. He is currently working with Los Angeles gang members
through his Amer-I-Can organization.

On the heels of Brown's successful transition in the 1970s,
Hollywood turned to other Black athletes to fill the screen roles
that audiences were demanding.

O. J. Simpson appeared in films like *The Klansman* and *The*

Towering Inferno in 1974, as well as appearing in several memorable Hertz rental car television commercials, and print ads for Dingo boots. Fred Williamson, a former defensive back for the Kansas City Chiefs, came to prominence in *Black Caesar* and its sequel, *Hell Up in Harlem*, and also starred with Brown in *Three the Hard Way*. Muhammad Ali starred as himself in the biopic *The Greatest*, while one of his nemeses in the ring, the former heavyweight champion Ken Norton, appeared in the blaxploitation slave melodramas *Mandingo* and *Drum*. Dr. J starred as basketball savior Moses Guthrie in *The Fish That Saved Pittsburgh* (1979). Carl Weathers, a former linebacker for the Oakland Raiders, had been in films like *Bucktown* (1975) and the Pam Grier vehicle *Friday Foster* before crossing over to the role that would forever define him, that of the boxer Apollo Creed in *Rocky* (1976). Weathers reprised the Apollo Creed character for *Rocky II* (1979) and *Rocky III* (1982) before being killed off in *Rocky IV* (1985). Bernie Casey, once a wide receiver for both the San Francisco 49ers and the Los Angeles Rams, gained recognition playing J. C. Caroline in the television movie *Brian's Song* before appearing in films like *Cleopatra Jones*, *Maurie* (1973), and *Cornbread, Earl and Me* (1975), which also featured NBA player Keith Wilkes, who would later change his name to Jamal Wilkes. Rosie Grier, the former Los Angeles Rams defensive lineman, who was serving as a bodyguard for Robert Kennedy when he was assassinated in 1968, was also the cousin of Pam Grier, and appeared in *The Thing with Two Heads* (1972); he also appeared with Casey in *Roots: The Next Generations*.

Perhaps the best example of the popularity of Black athletes in Hollywood was a film called *The Black Six* (1974), in which a group composed of six of the best NFL players of that era takes on a 150-member motorcycle gang. The film starred Gene Washington of the 49ers, Mercury Morris of the Miami Dolphins, Willie Lanier of the Kansas City Chiefs, Lem Barney of the Detroit Lions, Carl Eller of the Minnesota Vikings, and "Mean" Joe Greene of the Pittsburgh Steelers. The film's tagline said it all: "Six Times Tougher Than *Shaft*, Six Times Rougher Than *Super Fly*." *The Black Six* is arguably one of the worst movies ever made. It's the kind of the film that makes you happy that these six NFL stars had day jobs to go back to. But, in hindsight, the film is so bad that it's hilarious.

DARRYL DAWKINS

With the fifth overall pick in the 1975 NBA draft, the Philadelphia 76ers selected Darryl Dawkins of Maynard Evans High School in Orlando, Florida. Dawkins was the first player in history to go directly from high school to the NBA.

Moses Malone, the most successful player of his time to make the transition from high school to pro, and arguably the best player to date to make such a move, had been selected in 1974 by the Utah Stars of the now defunct ABA. Bill Willoughby, another high school player from Englewood, New Jersey, was selected in the second round of the 1975 draft by the Atlanta Hawks. After this spate of high school signings in the '70s, the

practice died until the Minnesota Timberwolves selected Kevin Garnett in 1995. Since that time, high school players going directly to the NBA has become commonplace. It was players like Dawkins, Malone, and Willoughby, however, who were the real pioneers in this regard. And though Malone would go on to have a far more distinguished career, it was Dawkins who made the biggest impact on the culture.

Dawkins, who went by the nickname "Chocolate Thunder," and claimed to have come from the fictional planet "Lovetron," was often referred to as a man-child by the media because of his youth and his six-foot-eleven-inch 250-pound frame. Chocolate Thunder was once quoted as saying that because he was so big, his birthday unfolded over three days. He is really emblematic of the '70s, and one could argue that he achieved icon status, much like his 76ers teammate Dr. J—but for very different reasons. Similar to the eclectic combo of the dignified, larger-than-life icon Michael Jordan and the outrageous Dennis Rodman of the Chicago Bulls in the mid-1990s, the cool Dr. J was like smooth R & B to Dawkins's edgy funk.

During this time Philly featured several other idiosyncratic players as well, including the man originally known as Lloyd Free, who legally changed his name to World B. Free because he considered himself a world-class talent. This team also included one Joe "Jelly Bean" Bryant, a mediocre player who would enjoy a second life as the father of current NBA superstar Kobe Bean Bryant of the Los Angeles Lakers.

Dawkins made history on November 13, 1979, when he two-hand dunked the basketball with such brute force in a game against the Kansas City Kings in the Kansas City Memorial Auditorium that he shattered the Plexiglas backboard of the basket. The sheer force of his dunk was such that it sent pieces of the shattered backboard flying all over the place, while Dawkins and the other players ran or ducked to avoid being hit. It was like a meteor shower of broken Plexiglas. Reports that night said that it sounded like a bomb had gone off in the arena. Bill Robinzine, the player for the Kings who got dunked on, was nicked by a piece of the Plexiglas. Urban legend says that a piece of the broken backboard even ended up lodged in Dr. J's famous Afro. The game had to be delayed as the officials at the arena searched to find a replacement.

Three weeks later, on December 5, Dawkins did the same thing again, this time on his home court in Philadelphia. Soon thereafter the NBA, realizing that Dawkins could do this pretty much whenever he wanted to, adopted breakaway rims that would collapse—but not break—upon impact, so as to avoid future disruptions. These broken backboards made Dawkins into a cult figure, and the legacy of these dunks would follow him throughout the rest of his career.

Dawkins, ever the colorful cat, and clearly inspired by Muhammad Ali's prediction of which round he would knock his opponents out in, gave names to all of his dunks. The first broken-backboard dunk in Kansas City was called "the Chocolate-Thunder-Flying, Robinzine-Crying, Teeth-Shaking, Glass-Breaking, Rump-Roasting, Bun-Toasting, Wham-Bam, Glass-Breaker-I-Am Jam." Other dunk names included "the Yo' Mama," "the Rim Wrecker," "the Go-Rilla," "the Spine-Chiller Supreme," "the Look Out Below," and "the In-Yo'-Face Disgrace."

The dunk has long been a signature part of the urban street style of play, and it increasingly became more and more visible as a part of the NBA during the 1970s. Dr. J's dunks and those of the Denver Nuggets' David Thompson, the two most stylish dunkers of the '70s, were like watching ballet, poetry in motion. On the other hand, watching Dawkins's dunks were like watching the Incredible Hulk knock down a brick wall with his bare hands.

In the 1980s the NBA revived the dunk contest, a staple from the old ABA, and players like Michael Jordan, Dominique Wilkins, Spud Webb of the Atlanta Hawks, and Cleveland's Larry Nance distinguished themselves with stunning displays of their artistic physical ability with the ball. In the contemporary game, players like Vince Carter of New Jersey and Josh Smith of Atlanta have both continued and expanded upon the tradition. Though Darryl Dawkins never won a dunk contest, his he-man dunks focused attention on that aspect of the game and made getting dunked on the worst form of humiliation an opposing player could ever suffer on the court. Mix all of this in with his colorful, funk-inspired personality and you have a true icon of the Super Fly '70s.

Acknowledgments

Once again it's on! Time to give a strong red-black-and-green shout-out to my fam and all my peeps. What it do?! Peace, love, and respect to: Edward and Mozelle Boyd, Patrick Smith, Gil Friesen, Rick Famuyiwa, Ken Shropshire, Brian Smith, David Was, Carl Fletcher, Brandon Martin, Albert Berger, Frank and Katherine Price. Peace to Katherine Vondy, Akua Murphy, and Wendy Sung for all your valuable assistance. Peace to my editor, the former J. Hill, now J. Talbert. Peace to my agent, Winifred Golden. Peace to all those people who have shown love to the Good Doctor in person or via e-mail. Peace to all my students, both formal and informal, who love to hear me spit this -ism. Peace to all of those Super Fly '70s muthafuckas who made it do what it do and gave me the source material for writing this book. Finally I say peace to all you playa haters, jacklegs, window-shoppers, and all other fake, simpleminded, Cat-in-the-Hat-ass clowns who got somethin' slick to say about a pimp. Keep my name out yo' mouth! Like T.I. said, "motivation/niggaz fakin'

only gonna inspire (motivation)/all your hatin' is fuel to my fire!"
One of these days I'll get out the game and give the rest of y'all a
chance. Until then, keep hatin' and I'll keep doin' what I do
best—getting on your muthafuckin' nerves with all my success.
I'm out.

One

Notorious Glossary

Afro Sheen blowout-kit 'fro: a perfectly cropped Afro aided by the popular hair care product

Benjamins: hundred-dollar bills

blaze up: to light a joint for the purpose of smoking

blow: cocaine

boy: heroin

butt-ass naked: total nudity

by hook or by crook: by any means necessary

can you dig it?: "do you understand and agree with what I am saying?"

cathouse: an establishment that features live sex shows

collabo: a collaboration

crib: one's home or place of residence

dap: clean, well dressed, also a handshake, can also be an acknowledgment

deuce-and-a-quarter: a Buick Electra 225

equal-opportunity lover: someone who sleeps with members of any and all racial groups without prejudice

fly: slick, cool, especially stylish

game recognize game: when one playa recognizes another, respect

gat: a gun, references Gatling gun

gentleman: heroin, see also "boy"

getting his freak on: wild sex, to have sex

getting their groove on: to do your own thing, also to dance

girl: cocaine, see also "blow"

ham samich: a Cadillac, see also "hog"

handkerchief head: a Black female Uncle Tom, refers to the role of Hattie McDaniel

ho house madam: a whorehouse manager

hog: a Cadillac

just tryin' to eat: to attempt to survive, to attempt to make money

kicked to the curb: to be dismissed or disregarded

leather piece: a leather coat or jacket

the life: short for the pimp life, the lifestyle of pimps and prostitutes

li'l shortie: a small child

Lord Jesus: a perm for men, popular '70s hairstyle said to resemble images of a blue-eyed Jesus Christ

lyin' low: to be invisible, to avoid being seen

the Man: those in power, the establishment

mandingo: a Black male stud, reference to sexual politics of slavery and the 1975 film by the same name

Money House Blessing: popular ghetto air freshener intended as a spiritual blessing that is used to mask the smell of marijuana

paper: money

permed: see "Lord Jesus"

pimped-out: especially elaborate, see also "tricked out"

pimp-slappin': to slap someone with the back of the hand

playa hatin': to actively dislike a particularly successful individual, jealousy

private dick: private detective

'70s heads: those particularly knowledgeable about the 1970s

signifiyin': an expressive verbal critique, to talk shit

slangin': selling dope, to sell

spittin' some game: to say things of relevance in a particularly engaging fashion

street cred: to be deemed credible by the rules of the underworld

talkin' cash shit: to rely on aggressive arrogance and hyperbole in one's conversation

tricked out: accessorized

tryin' to get some draws: attempting to have sex

underworld kingpin: a gangsta, dope dealer, or hustler of any stripe with a great deal of success and authority

vine: a stylish suit

wack: weak, empty of meaning, insignificant

watch your back: be careful, be aware

went out like a lame: to be defeated in a particularly embarrassing fashion

whip: a car

whuppin': a beating

Works Consulted

ACHAM, CHRISTINE. *Revolution Televised: Prime Time and the Struggle for Black Power*. Minneapolis: University of Minnesota Press, 2004.

BOGLE, DONALD. *Toms, Coons, Mulattoes, Mammies, and Bucks: An Interpretative History of Blacks in American Film*. New York: Continuum Publishing, 2001.

GUERRERO, ED. *Framing Blackness: The African American Image in Film*. Philadelphia: Temple University Press, 1993.

VINCENT, RICKEY. *Funk: The Music, the People, and the Rhythm of the One*. New York: St. Martin's Press, 1996.

WATKINS, MEL. *On the Real Side: A History of African American Comedy from Slavery to Chris Rock*. Chicago: Lawrence Hill Books, 1999.

Photography Credits

2 Courtesy of Mathieu Bitton Archives/www.candytangerine.com

30 Courtesy of Mathieu Bitton Archives/www.candytangerine.com

36 Courtesy of Mathieu Bitton Archives/www.candytangerine.com

44 Courtesy of Mathieu Bitton Archives/www.candytangerine.com

52 Courtesy of Mathieu Bitton Archives/www.candytangerine.com

63 Courtesy of Mathieu Bitton Archives/www.candytangerine.com

69 Courtesy of Mathieu Bitton Archives/www.candytangerine.com

98 Courtesy of Mathieu Bitton Archives/www.candytangerine.com

107 Courtesy of Mathieu Bitton Archives/www.candytangerine.com

118 Courtesy of Mathieu Bitton Archives/www.candytangerine.com

140 Courtesy of Mathieu Bitton Archives/www.candytangerine.com

160 Julian Wasser/Time Life Pictures/Getty Images

164 CBS Photo Archive/Getty Images

165 ABC-TV/The Kobal Collection

173 NBC-TV/The Kobal Collection

175 Bud Yorkin/Norman Lear/Tandem/The Kobal Collection

177 Cornelius-Griffey/Photofest

192 Jim Cummins/NBAE/Getty Images

ABOUT THE AUTHOR

TODD BOYD, PH.D., is the Katherine and Frank Price Endowed Chair for the Study of Race and Popular Culture and Professor of Critical Studies in the USC School of Cinematic Arts. He is an accomplished author, media commentator, producer, and consultant. Dr. Boyd, who received his Ph.D. from the University of Iowa, is highly regarded as one of the nation's leading experts on popular culture, and he is especially distinguished in this regard for his pioneering work on race, media, hip hop culture, and sports. His five books include *Young, Black, Rich and Famous: The Rise of the NBA, the Hip Hop Invasion, and the Transformation of American Culture* (2003), *The New H.N.I.C.: The Death of Civil Rights and the Reign of Hip Hop* (2002), and *Am I Black Enough for You?: Popular Culture from the 'Hood and Beyond* (1997). Dr. Boyd was a producer and cowriter on the Paramount Pictures film *The Wood* (1999).

Dr. Boyd's writings on popular culture regularly appear in the *Los Angeles Times,* and his articles have also appeared in the *New*

York Times, International Herald Tribune, and Chicago Tribune. He has appeared as a commentator on the leading network and cable television programs, including NBC Nightly News, The Today Show (NBC), CBS Evening News, ABC World News Tonight, The News Hour with Jim Lehrer (PBS), Good Morning America (ABC), The Early Show (CBS), and Biography (A&E), among many others. He has been featured in several HBO sports documentaries; these include Perfect Upset: The 1985 Villanova vs. Georgetown NCAA Championship (2005), Bill Russell: My Life, My Way (2000), and O.J. in Black and White (2002), for which he was also a consultant. He is a frequent presence on ESPN and a commentator for National Public Radio. Dr. Boyd's comments have also appeared in virtually every major newspaper and magazine in the country, including: the New York Times, Time, Newsweek, Chicago Tribune, the Washington Post, Los Angeles Times, USA Today, GQ, People, Vibe, ESPN: The Magazine, London Guardian, and Agence France-Presse. Dr. Boyd has done commentary for the DVDs for Super Fly, Uptown Saturday Night, and The Mack. He has also recorded an interview that will be part of the documentary feature on the 30th Anniversary DVD release of Roots.